THE GREAT BOOKS:

A CHRISTIAN APPRAISAL

VOLUME III

Identical with this volume:

THE GREAT BOOKS, VOL. I ($2.50)

THE GREAT BOOKS, VOL. II ($2.75)

THE GREAT BOOKS, VOL. IV ($2.75)

Published by the Devin-Adair Company

THE
GREAT BOOKS

A CHRISTIAN APPRAISAL

A Symposium on the Third Year's Program
of the Great Books Foundation

Edited by

Harold C. Gardiner, s.j.

Literary Editor of "America"

THE DEVIN-ADAIR COMPANY

NEW YORK

Foreword

THIS IS Volume III of the four-volume series *The Great Books: A Christian Appraisal*. It follows the scheme and the purpose of the first and second volumes, namely, to evaluate by the standards of Christian thinking the books which are selected for study by the Great Books Foundation. As Volumes I and II considered the first and second years' books in the Foundation's four-year course, so Volume III takes in order those used in the third year. The substantial success of those volumes, and the large measure of appreciation which has been accorded them have made it eminently worthwhile to prepare this volume and to project the fourth.

From time to time the Great Books Foundation has elected to "change books." Subsequent printings of these volumes will follow these changes when possible.

Introduction

I HOPE that I am not being entirely too sanguine when I say that I really do not feel that this third volume of studies in the Great Books needs an introduction. Those readers who know the series and who have been eagerly awaiting the appearance of this third volume will recall that in the Introduction to Volume I, the aims and goals of these studies were outlined. These aims and goals remain the same, and it would seem that the need for the studies has deepened as the Great Books courses have spread both in quantity and quality around the country.

There is, however, one purpose which must be served by this Introduction. That is to point out, as must be done as a matter of mere prudence, the books included in the third year's course which are on the *Index of Forbidden Books*. Such a specification is called for because it is only the part of fairness to Catholics who may be participating in the Great Books discussions. They should not be left with the feeling that they have, perhaps, been led into rashness or danger because they become interested in a Christian appraisal of the Great Books. And so, permit me to issue the caution that Locke's *Essay concerning Human Understanding* and Gibbon's *The Decline and Fall of the Roman Empire* are, in their complete form, on the *Index*. In other words, if a follower of the Great Books is so interested in these works as a result of his discussions on them that he feels impelled to read them in their fullness, he should obtain the necessary permission.

This duty having been discharged—and gracefully enough, I hope, not to irritate those who do not catch the purpose of the *Index*—I have but to hope that Volume III will function as happily toward making the Great Books discussions interesting and fruitful as, I fondly hope, the preceding two volumes have done.

HAROLD C. GARDINER

vii

Contents

THE GREAT BOOKS:

A CHRISTIAN APPRAISAL

VOLUME III

Aeschylus: Prometheus Bound

IT IS EXTREMELY COMMON to find, in the mythology of many peoples, highly imaginative stories explaining the origin of human civilization. These tales represent men at first devoid of even the rudiments of culture. They attribute all the earliest discoveries to a definite inventor; the culture-hero. Thus, any Greek could tell at once that Prometheus had taught mankind the use of fire, the basis of all human culture, and they knew that Palamedes had invented writing, the calendar, and the game of checkers. Prometheus and Palamedes being the foremost culture-heroes of the Greek myths, their exploits became famous in Greek literature.

Moreover, it is worthy of note that the stories relating the introduction of culture and its elements to men emphasize the tremendous risk incurred by the heroes; for, by stealing the elements of civilization from the gods and bringing them to men, they readily come into conflict with the gods. This, indeed, was the reason why Prometheus became an enemy of Zeus and every kind of torment was showered upon the benefactor of mankind.

The story of Prometheus occurs for the first time in the Hesiodic poems (about 700 B.C.), where two different myths are recounted. The first, found in the *Theogony*, tells how, at a meeting of gods and men at Mēkōnē, Prometheus deceives Zeus in regard to the allotment of the portions of sacrificial victims. On one side he arranges the meat, covered with a bladder, on the other the bones, wrapped in fat. Zeus intentionally chooses the bones, the portion which looks best, because the attempt of Prometheus to deceive the gods provides him with an excellent motive for withholding fire from men towards whom he is not favorably inclined. The purpose of the story, as the poet himself says, is to explain why "the race of men on earth burn the white bones [of the victims] to the immortals on fragrant altars." In other words, it is an aetiological tale explaining the general custom of offering only the inferior portions of the sacrificial victims to the gods. Moreover, the fact that Zeus sees through the ruse of Prometheus looks like a charmingly naïve attempt to reconcile an old folk tale, in which the god really was deceived, with the poet's own concept of divine knowledge.

The second myth, found both in *Works and Days* and in the *Theogony*, tells how Zeus, always mindful of the first trickery of Prometheus, "did not give the force of unwearied fire to wretched mortals." But Prometheus, again outwitting the god, steals "the far gleam of untiring fire in a hollow reed," and brings it to man on earth. We note again how one of primitive man's experiences is clothed in a mythological tale. In primitive society, where the only known way of making fire is by the friction of wood, fire can easily be conceived of as a property stored away, like sap, in trees, which must be laboriously extracted by rubbing two pieces of wood together. Thus, fire is really hidden in a hollow reed and comes out whenever the reed is rubbed with a fire stick.

The retaliation of Zeus consists in the creation of Pandora, the first woman, upon whom the gods must bestow their choicest gifts. According to *Works and Days,* in which the Pandora story is told more fully, Hermes brings the woman to Epimetheus, the foolish brother of Prometheus, who, though he had been warned by Prometheus never to accept any gift from Zeus, receives the "evil thing." Since then, man finds himself committed to a life of toil. The account of Prometheus' punishment by Zeus is given by the poet in the *Theogony*. The hero is bound in tight and unbreakable fetters, and a stake is driven through his middle. An eagle devours his liver, which is immortal, so that at night as much grows again as the bird has consumed during the day. Finally, the hero is set free by Heracles, who brings about a reconciliation between Zeus and Prometheus.

From the foregoing outline it is clear that the myth of Prometheus, as told by Hesiod, has all the earmarks of a naïve folk tale describing a contest between a cunning minor god and a powerful high god, a contest in which wit is matched against power. No moral issue is involved. The old myth is just an agglomeration of stories told to account for some ritual practice—the custom of offering only the inferior portion of the sacrificial victim to the gods—and for some fact of every-day life—the relationship of man and woman. The framework of the myth is a sequence of strokes and counter strokes in a contest between Prometheus and Zeus. Prometheus deceives Zeus in regard to the allotment of the portions of sacrificial victims. Thereupon Zeus devises sorrow for men by hiding fire. Prometheus steals it again for man. Zeus retaliates by giving men an evil thing; he creates woman. The creation of woman means for man a life of toil.

This rather trivial story, then, was the material Aeschylus had at his disposal when he conceived the idea of making Prometheus the central figure of a tragedy. In his hands the myth underwent a profound transformation. With a fine instinct for what lent itself to serious treatment and what did not, he dropped the undignified quarrel about the dividing of the sacrificial portions as well as the Pandora story with its coarse wit. Moreover, he altered entirely the character of Prometheus. Out of the astute trickster and petty thief of the Hesiodic folk tale, Prometheus became the friend and champion of mankind, to whom the most noble motives are attributed. Accordingly, the poet represented Zeus as the supreme tyrant, a misanthropic god, whose evil designs were thwarted by Prometheus in order to save mankind.

To put these two contrasting characters in still bolder relief, Aeschylus invented a story about Prometheus' conduct in the struggle of Titans with Zeus and the Olympic deities (ll. 199ff.). When the rebellion led by Zeus against Cronus started in heaven, Prometheus first tried to settle the dispute and to restrain the Titans from violence. But when the latter refused to listen to his proposals, he and his mother, the prophetess Themis, or Gaia, threw in their lot with Zeus. It was on his advice that the Titans were shut up in gloomy Tartarus. But Zeus, after the style of a tyrant, repaid Prometheus with ingratitude. After having vanquished his opponents, he divided the realm of nature between the different gods with no notice being taken of mankind. On the contrary, Zeus harbored the idea of blotting out the entire race of men and creating another in their stead. Prometheus was the only one who dared rise up against this injustice and thus save mankind from destruction. It is for this deed that he has to suffer dreadful torments.

Prometheus enumerates all his efforts on behalf of mankind: by spreading the merciful veil of uncertainty over the future and planting hopes in the hearts of men (this is the only relic of the Pandora story), he saved them from despair (ll. 250ff.); by giving them fire, he opened for them the way to many arts and crafts (ll. 254ff.). He lists them individually (ll. 442ff.): brick masonry, carpentry, astronomy, arithmetic, the art of writing, the taming of horses, navigation, medicine, the different methods of divination, the working of mines.

The great number of changes and additions to the traditional Prometheus saga explains the extraordinary length of the exposition in which Prometheus recounts the hitherto-unknown story of his rebellion against the Olympic deities and his efforts on behalf of mankind, a story which ends with the proud statement: "All human arts are from Prometheus" (l. 506). In this way the hero introduces himself as the benefactor of both gods and men: the former being indebted to him for their victory over the Titans, the latter for their salvation and for civilization, which was made possible by the gift of fire.

In no other Greek tragedy is there so much stress laid on the characterization of the hero before the action starts as in the *Prometheus Bound,* in which almost half of the play serves this purpose. As a matter of fact, the poet seems to be more interested in describing carefully and minutely this new type of tragic hero than in the action itself: he represents a god unreservedly benevolent toward mankind, who submits to the greatest sufferings on behalf of his protégés and for their sake makes the seemingly hopeless attempt at overthrowing the rule of the Olympians. He pictures both a hero of indomitable strength of mind and a god of extraordinary wisdom, whose most striking trait of character is love of mankind and justice. In this way he accomplishes his main purpose: all the feelings of sympathy are directed toward the new hero, while they are withheld from the brutal young victor over the Titans.

As a matter of fact, neither the Chorus nor Oceanus nor Hermes states, or even suggests, that Zeus in any way is in the right or led by good intentions; all they do is to caution Prometheus against coming into conflict with the unyielding self-will of Zeus and his superior power. Thus, the basic theme, as so often in Greek tragedy, appears to be the conflict between brute force and justice, a conflict at first sight apparently insoluble, in which man and his champion seem to be helpless against a tyrant god. The raising of this problem, however, should by no means be construed as an attack upon the old religion of Greece. Such an assumption is contradicted by the fact that, throughout the play, the idea that Zeus is new in the rule and that "conquerors are hard in the early days," is emphasized again and again.

This point is important, because it prepares for the final solution of the conflict Aeschylus seems to have proposed: a compromise between two opposites. Such a solution would also be in conformity with the dramatic method of Aeschylus, who frequently takes his subjects from myths that tell of a conflict on a cosmic scale, and finds the ultimate solution in the concessions made by both opponents. We have a somewhat similar conclusion in the *Oresteia*, where the old gods and the new are at last reconciled, and the final solution consists in tempering rigid justice with mercy.

However, before considering this solution, we must turn for a moment to the structure of the *Prometheus Bound*. Here, the poet was immediately confronted with a difficult problem. Since the protagonist is bound to a cliff throughout the play, and therefore motionless, the plot has extremely limited possibilities for action. Yet the play is by no means static; it moves without cessation.

Aeschylus obtains this result in two ways: by the dramatic development in the character of the protagonist, and by keeping the spectators in continuous and ever-growing suspense in regard to the future. The latter is accomplished by the introduction of a new motif, which consists in providing Prometheus with the knowledge of the famous secret on which the reign of Zeus depends. Gaia, the mother of the Titans, knows that Zeus is on the point of wedding Thetis. This matrimonial alliance, however, spells ruin to the new ruler, because it has been ordained by fate that Thetis shall bear a son who will overthrow his father. Prometheus learns the secret from his mother and thus possesses a weapon which, if he can only hold out long enough, will guarantee him his final triumph over Zeus. The motif of the secret undoubtedly endows the protagonist with vitality; without this weapon, he could only utter complaints and abuses. That the poet himself attached a great importance to the motif is clear from the fact that it appears at the end of each of the three marked pauses which divide the play into four movements.

In the first movement we witness the punishment of Prometheus by Zeus. Kratos (Might) and Bia (Violence), the two attendant demons of Zeus and true symbols of his tyrannical rule, have dragged Prometheus to a rocky gorge in Scythia. Though to Hephaestus the binding of a kindred god is repugnant, Zeus's cruel determination leaves him with no alternative. Reluctantly he binds Prometheus with chains to a high-ridged cliff. Being immortal, the Titan cannot be punished by death but only by torments, so a stake is driven through his chest.

The chaining of Prometheus is followed by his magnificent soliloquy, which gives the simplest statement of the situation. He is joined by the Chorus of sea nymphs who, in a moving song of compassion, sympathize with the sufferer. At the end of his dialog with the Chorus, Prometheus alludes for the first time to the mysterious secret in his possession which will unseat the tyrant.

In the second movement, the Titan recounts the struggle of the gods in heaven and his services to Zeus, and relates the story of his benefits to man. The Chorus manifests again its affection for the sufferer who, now for the second time, mentions the secret which will bring about his deliverance.

The third movement introduces a fellow sufferer of Prometheus, the maiden Io. The account she gives of her past sufferings, caused by Zeus's wanton lust, is singularly moving. Her story is continued by Prometheus, who predicts her further wanderings and ultimate fate. The scene is of great importance for the development in the character of the protagonist, because the appearance of Io brings about a profound change in the Titan. He now passes from mere dejection and stubbornness to bold assurance and defiance, alluding once more, but this time more explicitly and more ominously, to his enemy's downfall.

The climax of the play is reached in the fourth movement when, in the superb dialog between Prometheus and Hermes, the Titan, in blind rage, and abandoning every restraint, answers the threats of Hermes, the messenger of Zeus, with defiance and a point-blank refusal to reveal the secret. After a heated altercation, Hermes announces that a more severe punishment will be inflicted on the Titan. The ever-increasing tension and the approaching catastrophe are reflected in the impetuous anapaests with which the play comes to an end amid thunder and lightning, tempest and earthquake. Even the Chorus, hitherto so timid, is suddenly seized by Promethean spirit and disdains the salvation offered by Hermes. While Prometheus is plunged into the depth, he once more calls upon the powers he has invoked in his first monolog, as witnesses of the injustice he suffers.

This, then, is the situation at the end of the *Prometheus Bound:* the rebellion of the champion of helpless mankind has led to still greater injustice on the part of the tyrant god.

Obviously this cannot be the final solution of the problem propounded by Aeschylus. The Zeus of the *Prometheus Bound* differs so entirely from the Zeus of the *Oresteia* as well as from the Zeus of Aeschylus' own belief that a number of scholars have doubted the very authenticity of the play and assigned it to an unknown author of about the middle of the fifth century.

This theory, however, has not commanded general acceptance, and the *Prometheus Bound* is usually considered to have been the first play of a trilogy whose companion plays probably were *The Unbinding of Prometheus* and *Prometheus the Fire-Bearer.* There are about twenty references to the second play, treating the "unbinding," or release, of Prometheus, in ancient literature, so that we are in a position to form an idea of the plot. Two points seem to be especially worthy of note. The Chorus of the play is formed by the Titans who, like the daughters of Oceanus, sympathize with Prometheus. Zeus, therefore, must have pardoned and released them from Tartarus; he must have softened; he is no longer the Zeus of the *Prometheus Bound.*

Moreover, one of the characters of the second play is Gaia, the mother of the Titans, who has revealed to Prometheus the secret on which the fate of Zeus depends. She also is the one who, with the consent of Prometheus, can disclose the secret to Zeus and thus save him. This in turn gives Zeus freedom of action: now he can send his own son, Heracles, to kill the eagle and release Prometheus.

The content of the third play seems to have been the solemnization of the peace established between Zeus and Prometheus, the champion of mankind. As in the *Eumenides,* the third play of the *Oresteia,* the magnificent finale was the institution of a great ritual, the Prometheia. We know that the climax of that festival was a race in which the contestants carried lighted torches. Zeus has changed into a friend of mankind, and love of mankind becomes now the outstanding virtue of the gods. Thus, the ritual of the Prometheia also symbolizes, as it were, an agreement between the godhead and mankind: the spark of fire has not been conveyed in vain from heaven to earth; all the gifts of civilization can now develop. All Zeus requests from man in return is piety. But above all, Prometheus himself, the firebringer, is raised to the fellowship of the Olympian gods. In his honor, grateful men celebrate every year the festival of the Prometheia.

The fundamental problem of the Prometheus trilogy then appears to be similar to that of the *Oresteia* (cf. *The Great Books,* vol. II, pp. 20-24): how can the evil present in the world be reconciled with its Ruler, who is supposed to be all-powerful? Aeschylus solves the tragic problem of the *Oresteia* by the conception of the eventual reconciliation of all divine powers, the union of the old Fates with Zeus. As a result, the rigid and mechanical law of justice (Dikē) is tempered by reason and mercy, and Orestes is pardoned. A similar conception seems to be at the bottom of the Prometheus trilogy: the Titan finally makes his peace with Zeus. This is accomplished by the establishment of Zeus as a god not only all powerful but also all just after he had grown in age and wisdom. Before Zeus, the world was governed by blind and brutal forces. Zeus overpowers and imprisons them. Though, at the beginning, his rule is also tyrannical, something new comes into the world with him. He possesses a new and unique faculty: the power to think, to learn by experience. Thus, in the course of ages Zeus learns wisdom. This end has not yet been attained in the *Prometheus Bound.* Since the subsequent plays of the trilogy have been lost and the surviving fragments are too scanty, the interpretation, which admittedly can only be tentative, must be based on evidence from extant Aeschylean plays, which deal with essentially the same philosophical and religious problem.

No doubt, the idea of a maturing god, though consonant with ancient thought in general and Aeschylean thought in particular, is alien to Christianity. Not only does the Christian conception of God include His omnipotence, His holiness and His goodness, but these attributes are, as God Himself, absolute and exist from all eternity.

Man and the world, being of God's making, reflect in their very substance some of the Creator's greatness and goodness. The good things of the universe are from the very beginning meant for the enjoyment of man. Man need not wrest them from God but may progressively discover and use them. But he must recognize God as his maker and benefactor. Unfortunately, man has attempted the impossible, that is, to be independent of God. By this perversion of the will the very ontological order and purpose of the universe has been disturbed; the original harmony of the creation is distraught. Thus, evil has come into the world, which affects every sphere of being and activity, moral, intellectual and physical. By obstinately clinging to his wrong attitude, man imputes his handicaps and sufferings to an evil intent of God, or resorts to the materialistic explanation of the evil in the world as the painful upward struggle of blind evolution. The Christian recognizes his guilt and accepts the consequences of his own doing, while gratefully enjoying the benefits of the creation available to him. Thus, his mind is properly orientated toward the eternal goal of life, while he gives himself wholeheartedly to the searching out and enjoyment of the treasures of the world according to the plan of the Creator.

By the foregoing statement we do not belittle the great accomplishments of Aeschylus as a religious thinker. The poet was an heir to an anthropomorphic conception of the godhead. The gods of the Homeric religion, though they were immortal and far outclassed mankind in power, beauty and intelligence, also had human emotions and passions, and only too often did they exhibit human weaknesses. The fact that the gods stood in no fixed relationship with morality gnawed at the very nerve center of Greek religion. The Greeks, a really religious people, could not be satisfied with such a point of view. Their poets and philosophers stoutly struggled with this difficult problem. Aeschylus was one of them, and his interpretation of the Prometheus theme will always command the admiration of every serious reader.

We have mentioned the great influence the Prometheus legend

had on Greek literature. The myth was also interpreted by early Christian writers, for instance, Tertullian (about 200 A.D.), who calls God the "true Prometheus." Since, by its very nature, the Prometheus theme constitutes a challenge to the human mind, its treatment by modern poets is hardly surprising. The best-known attempts at a solution of the problem are Goethe's *Prometheus* which, however, remained a fragment, and Shelley's *Prometheus Unbound*. Finally, the most impressive interpretation is found in *The Book of Job*, which is discussed in another section of this volume.

RUDOLPH ARBESMANN

SELECTED BIBLIOGRAPHY

HARRY, Joseph Edward, *Greek Tragedy*, Vol. I: *Aeschylus and Sophocles*. Columbia University Press.
MURRAY, Gilbert, *Aeschylus: The Creator of Tragedy*. Oxford.
HARSH, Philip Whaley, *A Handbook of Classical Drama*. Stanford University Press.
THOMSON, George, "Notes on *Prometheus Vinctus*." *The Classical Quarterly* 23 (1929), pp. 155-163.
GRENE, David, "Prometheus Bound." *Classical Philology* 35 (1940), pp. 22-38.
AESCHYLUS, *Prometheus Bound. The Bible: The Book of Job*. Regnery.

The Bible: The Book of Job

HUMAN SUFFERING has been an ever-present problem for men in all ages. With the belief in God or gods almost universal in ancient times, the problem could not fail to raise the question of God's part in causing or permitting suffering. In the Book of Job the problem is stripped of all accidental elements by a keen mind acknowledged to be of the first rank in both thought and expression, the mind of a philosopher and a poet illuminated by the light of revelation.

Attention is focused on the essence of the matter by narrowing the question down to the just man. The notion of justice in the sufferer is fundamental, so it is made clear in the prolog (Chaps. 1, 2) that Job is acknowledged to be just and blameless not only by his fellow men but also by God Himself. This at once excludes any answer to the problem that is based on human wickedness, folly or carelessness. To make the issue still more clear, though the earlier evils that befall Job come from the violence of men, the later ones, the storm that kills his children and the disease that tortures his body, are due to forces that would be considered to be more directly under the control of God.

In the greater part of the Old Testament, God is seen as the just distributor of the blessings and woes of this life, and in this distribution He had to be guided by the individual's worthiness or unworthiness. The wicked are doomed to be soon stripped of their ill-gotten gains, the weak will be avenged against their oppressors, and happy always are they who are faithful to God, since He will reward them with a long, happy life in material prosperity.

This was the view of Job's friends and of Job himself before he was engulfed in misery. It could not be maintained, however, when confronted with Job's justness, once it was certain that his justness was real and not merely his own false estimate. Job's friends argue back from his suffering to a denial of his justness; since he suffers, he must be guilty. But for Job, conscious of his innocence, the question is why the just God afflicts him.

In the prolog, Job is a model of patience, resignation and filial trust in God. He leaves everything to Him: "the Lord has given and the Lord has taken away; blessed be the name of the Lord." But the arrival of his three friends and their silent condemnation brings him into a new field. Knowing their thoughts, Job gives free rein in Oriental style to the expression of his sorrow; it would have been better, he says, not to have been born than to endure such agony. In their attempt to console him, the friends follow the popular line, pointing out that repentance is the only way to recover happiness. The body of the book is the debate between them and Job as they defend the theory of punishment for sin while Job stoutly defends his innocence, refutes their arguments, and seeks in vain for another explanation. The divine attributes of omnipotence, wisdom, justice and goodness are held as true by all alike, though at times the friends accuse Job of asserting that God is unjust in making him suffer. The problem for Job is to reconcile these divine attributes with his misfortunes.

The skilful construction of the prolog should be stressed. The rapid enumeration of the series of evils, with the messengers reporting in almost the same terms, shows that the author is aiming at literary effect and not at historical accuracy. The heavenly court is described in a way fitted to the understanding of his readers. Satan, "the adversary," is not the spirit of evil as we know him but merely one of the angels whose duty it is to report on men's conduct when they stray. This adversary cannot deny Job's virtue, but he brings up the question of disinterested love. Throughout, emphasis is placed on the part played by divine providence in human affairs, and care is taken to impress the reader with the extremity of Job's suffering not only by the rapidity with which his losses succeed one another but also by the reprehension he has to bear from his wife.

The arrival of his friends adds immeasurably to Job's misery, since he knows what they think of his plight. He sets them talking by breaking forth into a loud lament. His vehemence here is intended to lay bare the agony of his soul, and it must be understood in the light of Oriental mentality, since, in the East, sorrow is judged mainly by the measure in which it is expressed. Stoical silence or moderate mourning would give the impression that the sufferer was only mildly affected and that consequently his woes must be quite tolerable.

When the friends offer their consolation and advice, Job's inner struggle increases. Since he is innocent, their explanation must be unsound, and Job hotly resents it. They insist on its truth, and both sides of the debate grow more vehement as the argument is prolonged; they draw up indictments of the sins they imagine he must have committed, and Job points to the obvious prosperity of many known sinners and of their posterity. Then comes the bitter accusation, logical enough on their theory, that Job is accusing God of being unjust. Though some of Job's protests might lend color to this charge, he loyally proclaims the justice of God, but he is still at a loss to account for his suffering.

In his distress he pleads with God to come to his aid. Are these pangs really due to God's hostility? Has he ceased to be the friend of God? If it is because of sin (the prolog has shown us it is not), let God make known his sin, since he is unaware of having offended. When the friends refuse to yield to the evidence which he offers to prove their explanation wrong, he can see no way out except through a personal interview with God. So, while admitting his nothingness in comparison with the infinite wisdom of God, he begs for a trial, with God presiding. If only he can lay his case before God with his friends looking on, he knows that the verdict will be in his favor.

With the debate closed, another figure takes the stage, Elihu, the representative of "flaming youth." Some find a new note sounded in his reference to suffering as a means of instruction (Chap. 33: 19-30), but the context indicates that he applies this to sinners and so, like the friends, he misses the point at issue. At the close, the voice of God is heard from the midst of the storm which had been gathering during Elihu's last speech. While God blames Job for speaking rashly at times, He approves his refusal to accept the solution of his friends. In token of His approval He restores Job to health and happiness and orders the friends to seek Job's intercession with Him.

This is an imaginative composition, but it is based on history.

The fictional character of most of the story is clear from the metrical structure of the speeches and especially from the prolog, with its artistic arrangement of the misfortunes of Job and with its picture of the heavenly court where the details are chosen to fit man's limited understanding of the other world.

But a rich man named Job did live in the land of Huss, a part of Arabia southeast of the Dead Sea, and he did meet with serious reverses which he bore with exemplary patience in spite of criticism. The author, a Palestinian Jew writing about 400 B.C., builds his drama on this bit of history, poetically conceiving the setting and development of the debate and trying to view the matter through the eyes of the actors and in the prolog, and the theophany through the eyes of God Himself.

The book is one of the world's greatest dramas, but the action is confined almost exclusively to the soul of Job. The actors do not move from their initial position—but the friends sit around Job, who in his dejection has seated himself on the public dump. But Job's soul, racked by pain and misfortune and tossed about by the accusations of his friends and by his own inability to find a solution for his problem, passes through a wide range of emotions—deep mourning, sharp resentment against his false consolers, helplessness in the presence of God, longing for death, praise of God and trust in Him, and through all a fierce and insistent desire for God's solution as his vindication.

It is only in the latest books of the Old Testament that revelation concerning the future life is introduced to explain man's suffering, and this revelation reaches its fulness only in the New Testament, where the teaching and example of Jesus Christ mark out the Royal Way of the Cross. Ordinary Catholic translations of the Bible, based on the Latin Vulgate, credit Job with expressing belief in the resurrection of the body and in reward after death (Chap. 19: 23-27), but the text is uncertain and the original Hebrew text, though obscure, is clear enough to exclude this explanation definitely and to keep Job's ideas and hopes within the present realm. Even if the Vulgate reading is retained, it would have to be discounted, because this clarifying idea could have been only a fleeting one to Job; it exerts no influence on the debate which continues on the previous lines.

The negative answer to the problem is obvious from the prolog, from Job's refutation of his friends, and from the closing speeches of God: the friends are wrong in attributing all suffering to personal sins. Positive contributions to the theory of human suffering are found first in the lesson of patient endurance given by Job at the start, a lesson explicitly noted in Tobias (Chap. 2: 12), and secondly in the insight given by the prolog into the designs of God. In Job's case the design was to give him the chance to prove that he could remain faithful even though God withdrew His temporal blessings. Job, of course, was unaware of this design, and under pressure of his friends he goes beyond prudence in insisting on getting an explanation from God. At the end, God blames Job for not understanding that man's part is to trust the wisdom, power and goodness of God with complete confidence and resignation and not to ask that the divine purpose be explained to him.

These divine designs will differ for different persons, but the universal application is that in inflicting suffering or permitting it to be inflicted, God has always a definite purpose—which includes the greater good of the one suffering. He neither lacks the power to ward off pain from His friends nor is He indifferent to it. He holds all things in His loving control and, as long as man cooperates and in the measure of that cooperation, He will bring good out of the seeming evil not only to others but also to the sufferer. Job is not merely restored to temporal prosperity; he comes out of the trial with increased knowledge and love of God and stands as a refutation of the sneering accusation that virtue is practiced only because of the material rewards it wins.

WILLIAM A. DOWD

SELECTED BIBLIOGRAPHY

KISSANE, Edward J., *The Book of Job*. Sheed & Ward.
O'NEILL, George, S.J., *The World's Classic, Job*. Bruce.
PRAT, F., S.J., "Job" in *Dictionnaire de la Bible*.
KNABENBAUER, J., S.J., *Commentarius in librum Job*. Paris: Pustet.
MOULTON, Richard G., *The Literary Study of the Bible*. Heath.
AESCHYLUS, *Prometheus Bound. The Bible: The Book of Job*. Regnery.

Plato: Symposium (The Banquet)

CHRIST HIMSELF has told us that love is the only commandment. And St. Paul has told us that when all things are past only love will remain. Therefore, love is the greatest of goals, the prime subject for discussion or discovery by philosophers, theologians and saints. It happens to be the total subject of the *Symposium*, the most colorful and brilliant of all the dialogs of Plato. And whatever his answer about the nature of Charity, it is perhaps the most refined analysis of this fairest of all objects by a non-Christian mind. Let us see how far the human mind can go without wings.

We have an infinitely controvertible affair on our hands as soon as we begin to discuss the genius of Plato (Socrates was his mouthpiece, and with the scholars we will leave unsettled which of the two said what). Whatever that genius was in reality, many have relegated him to the category of poet and thereby have left every philosophical word of the man open to suspicion. We like to regard him as a thinker of supreme but somewhat uncertain intuitions. Actually, he emerges in the history of philosophy as the great critic of intuition and as the first important pleader for an "examined," a philosophical, life, that will be as rational and defined in its goals as the human mind can make it.

So much is this true of Plato that he has just as often been dubbed the great enemy of imagination and existence and life. Nietzsche, in his *Birth of Tragedy*, has called Plato's Socrates the rationalist *par excellence* and the destroyer of Dionysus, of everything mystical and profound in man. George Grote has described the same Socrates as the great Sophist, the user of "reason" to the point of complete perversion. Nygren has blamed Plato for the introduction of a baser, rational element into "pure Christianity." And so it goes. At one moment we are given a

Plato who is the poet inserting nothing but a corrupting vague-
ness into the history of western philosophy; at another he is
described as the arch-analyst who, with his emphasis on concept
and definition, has devitalized the complicated and existential
man. Perhaps the best thing to do under the circumstances is
to stop reading the textbooks and to start reading Plato.

At any rate it is uniquely in the *Symposium* that this extraordinary human spirit breaks out into a glorious amalgam of both
vision and analysis as he seeks to track down the nature of love.
Outwardly, the dialog is a report of a true Greek symposium, a
banquet, a party of intellectuals, where enough drinking is done
to add extra fire to the conversation of some of the finest wits
of the Athens of 400 B.C. We are to suppose that Agathon is
there, fresh from a striking theater victory; Aristophanes, the
greatest of the Greek comedians; Euryximachus, the physician;
Pausanias, the Sophist, and Aristodemus and Phaedrus. Socrates,
the contemplative, enters only in the middle of the dinner. He
has become lost in thought on the way, and apparently no one
in Greece would disturb the thinker till he returned by himself
to earth. Alcibiades, the handsome but disastrous adventurer,
will break in at the end of things in a riot of fun and speech.
By that time there have been five discourses on love, climaxed
by the since-then-memorable epilog of Socrates himself. Let us
go back and listen to some of the talk.

Up until the minute when Plato will intervene through the
discourse of Socrates, what we have been given is a set of brilliant
intuitions and half guesses and rare hits and sanctified myths on
the nature of the fair God of Love. Only people in love will
agree to die for one another. Orpheus was no more than a
coward who would for love go down to Hades alive but would
not first consent to die. No human action is noble or ignoble
until the presence or absence of love comes to make it so. Love
is the principle, at the heart of all things, which establishes
health and harmony and rhythm between dissimilars and opposites and hatreds of all kinds. It is the power which, deriving
from an original unity and harmony in all, now tries to re-
establish the same ("of old we were one, but now because of our
transgression we are dispersed by God"). Of all virtues, love is
the most just, the most temperate and the bravest, delighting

in the beautiful, hating the ugly, a source of wonder to the wise and of joy to the gods.

To these flashes of insight that are drawn everywhere from Greek mythology and from medical and philosophical history, Socrates adds his now classical analysis. Briefly, there are two outstanding facets in his study: first, he looks at the human soul that is in love and tries to describe the "situation" of love. The result is a magnificent description of what the commentaries and courses that now derive in this country from European existentialism call "the human situation." In the second place, he understands that love can never be merely a subjective status or condition but must always have an object, must always be a desire *of something*. What Socrates thinks that object, that something, is will always remain as one of the sublime religious statements of non-Christian man.

The human situation! Pascal has described its essentially tragic nature, suffering fusion of aspirations and incapacities. Augustine had done the same far earlier than he, and the existentialists have done it far more recently—with their reaction against abstractions and their preoccupation with the actual condition of man in all its concretion. Heidegger and Sartre, the pagans among the existentialists, have pictured man as a sheer, irrational *project,* a thing that must of its very nature project itself endlessly beyond itself. And Goethe had said that sheer striving is the most blessed human thing. But in such men there is little or no talk of an object for our thirst. Even in Aristotle there is relatively little discussion of that which will sate the heart and give rest to all our motion. But Plato and Socrates have been so fascinated by the end and the goal of our searching that they have been accused of being unconcerned with the actual mud and bone and pity of our human state.

Nevertheless, here in the *Symposium* is the first elaborate philosophical picture of such things. Socrates tells us that love (he might almost have said *man*) is a midway thing, neither wise nor ignorant, neither good nor bad, neither beautiful nor ugly. Man exists and he is always in love with something. That is because he is as much a vacuum as he is a reality. It is because he is filled with a lack, with a lack of things which are good and somehow belong to him and which he desires to have with an eternal, unbreakable keeping. There is in him a poverty, a beg-

gary (which Aristotle would call *privation*). But he is not merely
poverty; he is not without a bridge to fulfilling. This bridge
is an inner drive toward the good; there is in him an inner
resource, which man cannot escape if he will and by which he
is constantly escaping out of himself and out of his poverty
(Aristotle would have called it an entelechy or a lack with a
sense of direction). And love is the child of this poverty and this
cunning, always caught in a thirsting, half-happy world, always
between filling and not quite being filled.

This drive toward the riches of fulfillment is also a drive
toward immortality—because we would have forever what we
desire. And thus all our acts of generation—in love, in thinking,
in writing—and all our search for fame are attempts to tie some
likeness or some memory of ourselves into the life or minds of
men for all time. It is our constant revolt against complete
poverty, against becoming nothing.

How then shall man break out of this undulating mountain
range of striving upward through the energy of love and falling
back into the lowliness of poverty? We must here carefully note
that the answer of Socrates to this question differentiates him
not only from the torturous seekings of the sensual man but in
certain substantial ways from the Christian as well. It is a magnificent answer but, like the love it analyzes, it is itself in the
tragic midway world to which all pure humanism dedicates itself.

First of all, its description of the object that will satisfy, and of
the process that will lead from tragedy to salvation is based on
the famous concepts of the *ladder* and the *ascent*. And these are
themes which will forever after break out into the writings of
such disparate saints as Augustine and Ignatius of Loyola and
Bonaventure. *They* will know how to Christianize this human
reaching. But such themes will in turn become subject to denun-
ciation by occasional non-Catholic theologians who are afraid
of humanism and of locating in man *any* power by which he can
save himself.

For Plato, the soul in love will be faced with many "im-
mediacies," with many fascinating objects that strike the eye
and ear with a compelling and immediate summons. There is
beauty in them, but he warns us that we must abide in none of
them. They are trifles that must be used and despised—their
function is to lead onward. The beauty in any one thing is part

of the beauty that is in all, and it is this eternal, reflected beauty we must always seek, while avoiding an endless number of possible slaveries. The search must ever be widened and deepened. Thus we shall go from one fair thing to all fair things in the sensible world, from the beauty of bodies to that of souls, then on to that of moral actions, to the beauty of all branches of knowledge, and finally to that one thing which breathes into and invigorates them all—which is eternal, neither begins nor ends, neither grows nor wanes, which is the totality of the beautiful, without any stain in it. This alone it is which will make life truly worth the living. It is the final object of all our toil.

Such is the doctrine which forms the substance of our dialog, a doctrine which Socrates, perhaps to heighten its splendor and mystery, imagines to have been communicated to him by a "Mantinean woman of Diotima," a name savoring of prophecy and of contact with God. Finally this figure turns to him, the teacher and intellectual midwife of Athens, and says:

What if it were the lot of one of you to behold absolute beauty entire, pure and unmixed with aught else, untainted by the flesh and color of humanity and all other kinds of human nonsense? What if he could behold the divine beauty itself in its purest form? Do you think it would be a small sort of life for a man to lead if he could look upon that and observe it as he should and consort with it? Or do you not suppose that in such case alone it will happen to him who sees the beautiful through that by which it becomes visible that he will generate not an imitation but the very reality of virtue? Will he not be laying hold of the truth and not quackery? And when he has begotten a true virtue and nourished it, he will become dear to God. If it belongs to any man to be immortal, it belongs to such as him.

But alas, all this seems like an impossible achievement for man—and surely it is. There is much nonsense in the charge that politically Plato was an aristocrat, but in his way of salvation there does lurk the great error of the aristocrat. A number of Christian thinkers like Scheler and Laberthonnière have charged that the love of Plato is at best a sublime form of intellectualism; indeed, it would seem that such a path is open only to the intellectual, and God help the people if this is salvation. Moreover, even to the intellectual the path to that which is the essence of all beauty is closed and he cannot break through.

St. Paul himself was later to pose the same problem with his "Who shall deliver us from the body of this death?" His answer was: only the grace of Christ. Only let us remember that His is a grace which abandons nothing that is human and need omit nothing in the humanistic ascent of Plato, but rather makes it all possible and leads to the final vision of love. Perhaps we should say "gives" rather than "leads." For this final thing is a pure gift, beyond all our energies and all our strivings.

We shall not say that Plato had even an inkling of this. For his doctrine of God and of man makes us hesitate to think that he could have guessed at the true nature of the supernatural. For him, God is a God to be contemplated—more of an object or thing than a Person—and not to be communicated with in an exchange of love. And his man is a Socrates whom Alcibiades pictures in the last pages of the *Symposium* as impeccable and strong. Such a man, it is true, needs God, but we have the impression he is strong enough to find Him. Whereas, the love of the saint knows that it needs the Love of God.

Yet even here one thing distinguishes Plato from Aristotle. The latter was always a bit of a dogmatist, where Plato was more modest in his thinking. Even as early as the *Phaedo,* Plato had said: these are our thoughts, and on this raft we shall swim—until some god reaches out and gives a better.

WILLIAM F. LYNCH

SELECTED BIBLIOGRAPHY

BURY, R. G., *Symposium of Plato.* Heffer.
COOPER, Lane, *Plato: Symposium,* translations into English. Oxford.
ANDERSON, F. A., *The Argument of Plato.* Dent.
TAYLOR, A. E., *Plato, The Man and His Work.* Dial.
SHOREY, Paul, *What Plato Said.* Chicago.
STEWART, J. A., *The Myths of Plato.* Macmillan.
PLATO, *Symposium.* Regnery.

Aristotle: Politics, *Books III-V*

ABOUT THE TIME that Confucius and Laotze taught in China, when the Persian despotism ruled the Near East, when the teeming millions of India accepted the religion of Gautama, and when the Jews, returning from the Babylonian captivity, rebuilt the Temple in Jerusalem—about that time the smallish City-state of Athens and her sister cities in that little peninsula called the Land of the Greeks, began to flourish and to extend their civilization by the founding of city-colonies in the coastal regions of Asia Minor, Sicily and Southern Italy. In contradistinction to most peoples who lived in the musty air of a despotism that claimed a spurious divine right, the Greeks introduced the first forms of a sort of democratic constitution, basing the life of the city upon the cooperation and self-determination of the free citizenry. They did not form a nation-state at that time. The City-state, or Polis, was the geographic limit of political life. Beyond the Polis there existed only loose confederations of such City-states, with restricted competencies and aims.

The Polis contained the City itself, built around the market place (agora), with the public buildings, and included the surrounding countryside with the rural suburbs and the farms, fields and vineyards. If the City was near the sea, there was a harbor sector as well. The amount of trade, though small, was enough to make the Polis an economically as well as a politically self-sufficient community.

The Polis embraced the citizen wholly: it was a State, a sovereign body politic; it was a "church," insofar as it had its own gods who were worshiped publicly; blasphemy of the gods or of the public religion was equal to treason. This produced a certain intolerance, of which the condemnation of Socrates for contempt of public religion (*asebeia*) is the most famous example. Anything resembling the modern separation of State and Religion was unthinkable, despite often-outspoken agnostic scepticism. Since the citizen belonged wholly to the Polis and was considered a man only because he was a citizen—he who was not a citizen (said a famous sentence) was either a demi-god or a barbarian— the idea of the rights of the person against the Polis and its all-comprehensive competency was taught only by the revolutionary-minded sophists and was despicable to Plato and Aristotle. Consequently, the Polis smacked somewhat of totalitarianism.

The inhabitants of the Polis consisted of free citizens, among whom the "old families" excelled, and often also of the *nouveaux riches*, the traders, manufacturers and ship owners. As a rule, one became a citizen only by the *jus sanguinis*, by birth from citizen-parents. The middle class consisted of professional men, shop-owning artisans, retailers—many of whom owned slaves. A wage-earning class, the lowest stratum of free citizens, was not numerous and found little esteem. The influence of the various strata showed itself in the respective constitutions: oligarchy, rule of the wealthy; aristocracy, rule of the "old families"; democracy, rule of all the freemen on the basis of equal political rights.

The Polis was comparatively small, more a town than a modern city, if only for the reason that in the *Ecclesia*—the town meeting or assembly in the market place—all citizens were meant to participate in the form of direct democracy; for representative democracy was practically unknown. Athens had, at the time of its Golden Age under Pericles (d. 429 B.C.), about 25,-000 citizens, to whom must be added the women and children and about 80,000 slaves, plus some 1,000 alien residents, the most famous of whom later was Aristotle himself.

The political development of the Polis started, according to tradition, with kings. They lost more and more of their power to the old families, thus giving way to an aristocracy. The aristocracy was superseded by more democratic forms of government which, being unstable, grew into tyrannies or oligarchies; these in turn were overthrown by successful democratic revolts of the broad mass of common citizens. Political life was certainly lively and full of changes in the Polis, at a time when the peoples of the Near East lived passively and dully under their despots.

Two outstanding types of the City-state developed: the military state of Sparta and the free, "democratic" republic of

Athens. Sparta's regime was authoritarian; its prototype was the always-ready army. Education, wholly subject to the "State," was predominantly military for boys as well as for girls. The men lived in barrack communities and ate in their messes. In the absence of war, their main task was policing the great mass of *helotes,* or slaves, who did the menial work in the city, and the *perioeci* (the rural peasantry), who worked the farms of the citizen-soldiers and small tradesmen. A Senate (council of old men), under the presidium of two "kings," was the supreme legislative body. It needed for passage of its resolutions the affirmative vote of the citizens' assembly, which, however, was excluded from all discussion and amendment.

Sparta originally had some socialistic features. Only immovable private property was countenanced; each citizen owned an entailed lot of land of equal size, worked by serfs. Sparta's coins were of iron. The citizens gained their livelihood by hunting and looting in war, and from the labor of their rural serfs and slaves. The stability and simplicity of their constitution and the strictness of their legal order, similar to that of an army camp, were often transfigured in a romantic way by Greek (Xenophon) and Roman (Plutarch) writers, and even Plato extolled Sparta as against the insecure order of the Athenian democracy, which was disturbed by party struggles and haunted by demagoguery.

The City-state of Athens based itself, after Solon's constitutional reforms, much more on freedom integrated with the self-responsibility of the citizenry. Athens is a prototype of direct democracy, with almost equal access of all to state offices. All citizens participated actively in the government as voters, electors, members of the Council and members of the Courts. Naturally, the danger endemic to such democracy—hidden rule by wealthy citizens, party bosses and party clubs, and demagoguery, with consequent instability of public order—were acutely enough experienced in Athens.

Yet, in spite of these drawbacks, it was Athens that represented the glory of Greece, and it was here that these noble minds, Plato and Aristotle, citizens, the one by birth, the other by adoption, taught their chosen students and wrote their imperishable treatises on Politics. It was in Athens that the "Legacy of Greece" was shaped, to become the formative power in our western civilization, a power not abrogated but transfigured and perfected by Christianity.

We must shy away from an identification of modern and Greek democracy. The latter was built upon slavery, which, for the Greeks, with the exception of some sophists, was a "natural" institution. The slaves did not participate in the good life. That, as the end of the State, was the privilege of the free citizens. Furthermore, it was a democracy of men; women, children, serfs, aliens who could never regularly be naturalized, were excluded from all political activity and from all offices. Since the Polis was small and the number of citizens restricted (the ideal polis should not have more than 10,000 citizens), Athens was an immediate democracy, the citizens meeting together in the market place in a town meeting. Almost everyone knew everyone else present. Ernest Baker compares the Polis quite properly to a large club (*Greek Political Theory*, Oxford, 1918, p. 19). With religion a part of the Polis, with education considered mostly an exclusive affair of the Polis, with Polis theaters and the Polis as the patron of the arts, it could be said of the Polis what Mussolini said of the State: nothing without the Polis, everything in and under the Polis.

For the Greeks, then, the idea of a sphere of private life staked out by a Bill of Rights against the government was hardly conceivable. For the Greek, the Polis was State and Church, Educator and supreme moral Authority, Arbitrator in all social-economic affairs; if times were bad for him individually or collectively, the Polis was the comprehensive welfare agency to which he turned for support. It is true that Socrates appeals, against the statutes of the Polis, to that inner voice that warns him against evil acts; but when, innocently condemned to death, he is offered escape from the prison into exile, he says that he must obey the laws, the "Nomoi," even if unjust men have applied them wrongly.

Against this background of the all-comprehensive bearing of the Polis on Greek life, it is easily understood why political life, constitutional law as a true way of life, the end, the nature, and the best or ideal form of government became from the very beginning one of the most urgent subjects of philosophical examination. So true was this that one could almost say that philosophy in Greece centers on political philosophy or the science of politics—not in an abstract and personally indifferent way, but in a spirit of personal and passionate concern.

As a youth, Plato wanted to go into politics. When he was disgusted by his experience he did not retire into an ivory tower but studied and, in his dialogs, taught the ideal form of the Polis. He traveled to Egypt, to Southern Italy, and to Syracuse, in Sicily, where he had as his student Dion, the brother-in-law of the tyrant Dionys I. He hoped to establish the ideal state through Dion. But the Tyrant had Plato arrested and sold as a slave in Aigina, where the wealthy Cyrenaen Annikeris recognized and redeemed him. Twice again did Plato return to Syracuse (367 and 361 B.C.) but without accomplishing anything. Aristotle, the friend of Hermias (a successful businessman and tyrant who afterward became, under Aristotle's influence, the constitutional ruler of Atarneus, a small Greek town near the ruins of Troja), was also the tutor of Alexander the Great and, in his late years, a private councillor to Antipater, the governor of Philip of Macedonia in Athens.

Aristotle, the son of a physician, was born in 384 B.C. at Stagira, a Greek settlement to the east of modern Saloniki. In 367 he went to Athens and became a student at Plato's Academy, a school of philosophy as well as of practical politics. After finishing his apprenticeship, at the end of which he had already criticized Plato's philosophy and had begun to conceive his own, Aristotle left Athens (Plato had died in 347) and went to Assus, in the neighborhood of Atarneus near the ruins of Troy in Asia Minor. There, with other disciples of Plato, he conducted a colonial academy, taught, and discussed with his colleagues the Philosophy and Politics of Plato's last work, *The Laws*. He became a friend and advisor to Hermias, who gave him his niece and adopted daughter as wife. After two years (344 to 342) in Mytilene on Lesbos, studying biology and marine life, he was called by Philip of Macedonia to Pella, the capital, to act as tutor to the Crown Prince Alexander, whom he educated from his thirteenth to his nineteenth year.

In 335, his "journeyman years" were ended, and he returned to Athens, a "master" in a particular sense. Here he opened his own school, the Lyceum, a kind of garden house (the spacious rooms of which served as library and classrooms) surrounded by a large garden and a walk (*peripeton*). Here Aristotle strolled while teaching his pupils (hence the word "peripatetic" to designate Aristotelian philosophy). At the Lyceum he wrote and composed in the form of lectures (using older notes and as new material his collection of 158 constitutions) the eight books of his *Politics*. This treatise is part of the great legacy of Greek thought to mankind; its wisdom and scientific penetration still capture the mind today.

The eight books of the *Politics* do not form a technically perfect work. They are lectures given at different times, but all relate to the central theme of the Polis, its origin, nature, end and constitutional forms. There often occur long digressions into particular problems which somewhat disturb the clear construction of the chapter or book; or, as in the case of Book III, the last chapter may end in the middle of a sentence that refers to the subject matter of Book VII. It seems that Aristotle did not polish up this great work. Books I and II give first a genetic development of the State from the family in its various aspects (e.g., as an economic unit) and of slavery as a "natural" institution. Book II reviews the "ideal States" of Greek thinkers and especially criticizes Plato's ideal state. Book III deals with citizenship and constitutions in general theory, while Books IV and V, typical of Aristotle's realism, study actual constitutions and the causes of their corruption and revolutionary changes. Book VI is concerned with Democracies and Oligarchies in particular, and Books VII and VIII with Aristotle's idea of the best state in all aspects.

The *Politics* of Aristotle, like his other works, reveals the characteristics of his philosophy, which in its full development in Aristotelian Thomism has been fittingly called "the educated twin-sister of common sense." Aristotle, though a pupil of Plato, rejected the latter's Idealism, that is, the doctrine that the sensible world of our daily experience is only a shadow, transparent only to the philosopher's trained mind that sees through it into the only real world in which the pure ideas dwell, the ideas of the true, the good, the beautiful, the ideas of the best state, the ideal justice, the true judge, etc. Aristotle considered what Plato called "ideas" to be the inner form and essence of the individual things in the world. Things are what they are by being realizations of the form, the nature, of the thing; they reach their perfection, therefore, when the mind realizes as perfectly as possible in the concrete their form, their nature, which is thus the end of their becoming, of their being formed under man's activities.

Hence, the observation and study, from all angles, of the world and the things in it (including the body politic) in their concrete reality, becomes of prime importance. We must observe the multitude of constitutions and forms of government of real cities; after the collection of facts, we can derive from them, by the process of abstracting from all particulars and nonessentials, the form, the idea or nature which is common to all of them in various degrees of perfection. The form then becomes also the end, that is, the purpose of our acts and their norm and yardstick.

A law is good insofar as it realizes the end of the State. This is the *realism* of Aristotle; it made him first collect as many facts as possible, and these then became the material from which the active critical mind abstracts the universal and necessary essence that is the truth of things. But this "realism" means also that the recognized truth becomes the rule of action. Therefore, politics, as Aristotle points out at the end of his *Ethics* (Book X, Chap. 9) is the continuation of ethics; the legislator must be a student, nay, a master, of ethics because it is the end of the Polis to lead man to his end, the good life of wisdom and virtue which consists in the search for truth and the tranquil possession of it. In this "good life" all the sciences harmonize like an orchestra. Politics is, then, for Aristotle, not an indifferent collection of facts, their classification, and the search for their relations in the spirit of a morally indifferent positive science. Politics is purposeful; it is an attempt to know in order to construct or at least help construct the best state, or the best constitution adapted to a particular Polis. Politics, as a practical science, tells us how we may, in our quality as citizens and statesmen, actively build (politics is also an architectural art) our community on the basis of ethics.

These were the features that made the great minds of medieval scholasticism, especially St. Thomas Aquinas, see "The Philosopher" in Aristotle. Natural human reason had reached its acme in him. Yet, certain features of Aristotle's political thought had to be rejected by Christianity. First, the Polis could no longer be that closed, all-embracing pedagog of men. Christ had founded His Church with its own end, its own visible body and divine law. Man lives in two cities now: in the City of Man for the temporal common good in the secular order, and in the City of God for his salvation as a member of the People of God; now man belongs only partly to the Polis, to the State, which is essentially limited. Secondly, the Christian person knows that the power of the Polis is restricted internally by the idea of the natural rights of the person and of the family, *i.e.* the rights of the parents *against* the State. Thirdly, the highest act of man on earth is not to gaze at the wonders of the world without and within; it is the contemplation of God, through Faith, who reveals Himself as Love. Thus, the Polis is transcended by the Church and by the Christian person working for his salvation by serving God. Fourthly, there is still a gleam of God's majesty on the State because it, too, has its place and function in God's creation and providence. But the state is a partial end now; it becomes the servant of man, who is called to a higher status than to citizenship in the city of man—in Christianity the Saint, no longer the wise man or the philosopher, is the exemplary figure. Fifthly, Aristotle's Polis was economically as well as philosophically built upon the institution of slavery. Certainly Aristotle shows a very humane attitude to slaves generally, and to his own house slaves particularly. Yet, though he may have had an uncertain conscience about it, he still defends the institution of slavery. He could not break down the barrier between Greek and Barbarian (naturally a slave), that is, between free citizen and slave.

We had to wait for Christianity to teach us the supernatural brotherhood of men, who are all called to the City of God. We had to wait for the Church, in which there are neither Greeks nor Barbarians, free men nor slaves, but where all are children of God and Brethren of Christ, Who redeemed all. The idea of a common brotherhood, which necessarily leads to the doctrine that all are equal and have inalienable rights, became effective through Christianity—and must die again when Christianity and its Gospel of Love, its *agape,* is forcefully oppressed, as is being done in our times by the totalitarian state.

HEINRICH ROMMEN

SELECTED BIBLIOGRAPHY

BARKER, E., *The Politics of Aristotle*. Oxford.
JAEGER, W., *Aristotle*. Oxford.
JAEGER, W., *Paideia: The Ideals of Greek Culture*. Oxford.
McILWAIN, C. H., *The Growth of Political Thought in the West*. Macmillan.
NEWMAN, W. L., *The Politics of Aristotle*. Oxford.
ZIMMERN, A. E., *The Greek Commonwealth*. Oxford.
ARISTOTLE, *Politics*. Dutton (Everyman's Library).
ARISTOTLE, *Politics*. Regnery.

Euclid: Elements of Geometry, *Book I*

THERE CAN BE no doubt that *Euclid's Elements,* as his book on geometry is called, truly ranks as one of the great books of all time. When we consider that the life span of even the most successful modern textbook is measured in decades, we cannot but be impressed by the fact that *Euclid's Elements* has served as a textbook in geometry for more than twenty centuries. The elementary texts used today are all merely adaptations of Euclid. They are intended for the young and are not too much concerned with rigor. Euclid wrote for mature people and wrote with all the rigor that was possible three centuries before Christ.

Geometry is a deductive science. Since it is a science, the propositions it contains must be related. Since it is a deductive science, the relation between the propositions must be one of dependence: one proposition must follow from another or from several others. Obviously not all propositions can be proved. Hence there must be some fundamental propositions incapable of proof. Euclid calls some of the fundamental propositions postulates, others he calls common notions. He lists five postulates and five common notions. The distinction is not too clear, but an examination of his postulates and common notions seems to indicate that the former are geometrical propositions, the latter more general propositions which apply to other fields besides geometry.

In addition to his fundamental, unproved propositions, Euclid lists twenty-three definitions. Most of these definitions explain geometric terms such as quadrilateral, circle, triangle, etc. and are still in common use. Others make an attempt to define the elements with which geometry is concerned, namely point, line, plane. Now it is just as impossible to define all the terms of a science as it is to prove all of its propositions. Some must be left undefined. Since point, line and plane are the elements of

which geometry treats, it seems natural to leave them undefined
and to define all other terms directly or indirectly in terms of
these elements. Strictly speaking, of course, these undefined elements are not really undefined, since their fundamental properties are listed in the postulates. To attempt any direct formal
definition may introduce new properties not listed in the postulates. This would offend against logical order by confounding
the purpose of definition and postulate. If Euclid's purpose in
attempting these definitions was to give his readers an intuitive
idea of what he meant by point, line and plane without ascrib-
ing to them any properties not contained in his postulates and
common notions, his procedure is not open to criticism. Modern
treatises on geometry which make any claim to logical rigor
leave these terms undefined.

Euclid has the distinction of having put geometry on a solid
foundation and of having given the world its first model of a
strictly deductive science. Nevertheless, there are imperfections
in the work of Euclid, though they were not discovered until
comparatively recent times. And so subtle are these imperfections that it required the combined work of hundreds of mathematicians working for centuries to bring them to light.

One of the more serious defects in Euclid's work is his use
of tacit assumptions. A classic example of this occurs in his sixteenth proposition: "In any triangle, if one of the sides be produced, the exterior angle is greater than either of the interior
and opposite angles." The proof he gives can be applied to
spherical triangles, of which the proposition is not always true.
The logical error in the proof is the tacit assumption that lines
are infinite. If that assumption is made explicit, then Euclid's
proof is valid. The distinction between unbounded but finite
and unbounded and infinite is not found in Euclid. A line segment is bounded, its bounds are the end points. A line which
extends to infinity in both directions is unbounded and infinite.
A segment of the circumference of a circle is bounded by its
end points. If this segment is extended so as to include the whole
circumference, there will be no end points. Hence it is unbounded though obviously finite. If an unbounded, finite line,
say a circle, is revolved through an angle of one hundred and
eighty degrees about a diameter, it generates the surface of a
sphere, a two-dimensional manifold, unbounded but finite. We

have no experience of any bounds of the universe, and this is a valid reason for believing the world unbounded. It is not a sufficient reason for believing it to be infinite.

Again, in proving some of his propositions on congruent triangles, Euclid uses superposition. Hence he assumes, and the assumption is implicit and not explicit, that figures can be moved about without distortion. If we recall that according to modern physics the length of a rod in motion is not the same as its length when at rest, and if we remember that physical bodies can rarely be displaced without suffering some distortion, we see the need of some sort of explicit assumption to justify the process of superposition. A better procedure would be to eliminate superposition entirely and arrive at the required propositions by other means.

There are still other tacit assumptions which Euclid makes. Mathematicians such as Pasch, Veronese, Peano and Hilbert have studied the problem of the foundations of geometry and have supplied the deficiencies left by Euclid. Perhaps the best-known set of postulates of Euclidean geometry is that of Hilbert. He lists eight postulates of connection, four of order, six of congruence, one of parallels, one of continuity, and one of linear completeness. Thus, the five postulates and five common notions of Euclid have grown into twenty-one postulates. With these, modern mathematicians are satisfied. They put Euclidean geometry on a firm foundation.

We may ask the question: how did Euclid view his postulates and common notions? Did he look upon them as self-evident truths, or did he view them as reasonably accurate approximations to the space of every-day experience? All the evidence seems to be in favor of the former view. The ancients cultivated truth, and for them a proposition was not true unless there was an extramental reality of which the proposition was verified. They were interested, of course, in logical consistency, but much more in learning about the real world in which they lived. For them, geometry was a study of the spatial relations of real objects in a real world. Again, unless the fundamental propositions are true and not merely approximations to the truth, we have no assurance that they are consistent. But if they are inconsistent, they must inevitably lead to contradictions. But nowhere is Euclid troubled by even a suspicion that his fundamental propositions might be inconsistent. Finally, for Euclid and all the ancients there was but a single geometry. They had no slightest suspicion that there might be others and that these others might differ essentially from the geometry they knew.

The non-Euclidean geometries owe their origin to the continued criticism of Euclid's fifth postulate, criticism which began in the days of Euclid and continued down the centuries. The fifth postulate reads: "That, if a straight line falling on two straight lines makes the interior angles on the same side less than two right angles, the two straight lines, if produced indefinitely, meet on that side on which are the angles less than the two right angles." It must be admitted that this postulate is much less simple than his other postulates. It can, of course, be replaced, but none of the substitutes offered is any simpler or more obviously true. Here are two of them: a) given any three points not lying in a straight line. There exists a circle passing through them; b) if three of the angles of a quadrilateral are right angles, then the fourth angle is also a right angle.

Many mathematicians tried to prove Euclid's fifth postulate directly as a proposition from the other postulates. Some of the proofs offered were exceedingly plausible, and it required mathematical talent of a high order to uncover the fallacy which they contained. All such efforts were foredoomed to failure, for we now know that Euclid's fifth postulate is independent of the rest.

The Jesuit Girolamo Saccheri (1667-1733) was the first to attack the problem from a different angle. He set out to prove Euclid's fifth postulate indirectly in his book *Euclides ab omni naevo vindicatus.* The book was published in 1773 in Milan and remained unnoticed. It was discovered in 1889 and republished with an English translation of the first part by Halstead. It is a remarkable book, for it gave the world its first glimpse of many of the propositions of non-Euclidean geometry fully one hundred years before the discovery of these geometries.

Saccheri began by considering an isosceles quadrilateral whose base angles are right angles. If Euclid's postulate is the only possible postulate, then the other two angles are also right angles. He easily proved that the other two angles must be equal. He then assumed that they were obtuse angles, and he sought to find a contradiction. Since with Euclid he tacitly assumed that straight lines are not only unbounded but infinite, he easily found the required contradiction. If he had not made this tacit assumption, no contradiction would have been forthcoming. If, in addition, he had realized that no contradiction was possible, he would have been the discoveror of what is now known as Elliptic geometry.

Having disposed of the case of the obtuse angle, he next assumed that the two remaining angles were acute. The contradiction which he confidently expected to find as a result of his assumption proved to be exceedingly elusive. The best he could do was to show that if the angles were acute, then the two lines produced to infinity would meet and there have a common perpendicular. As we read the text of Saccheri, we get the impression that he realized that he was not convincing his readers and that he was not quite convinced himself. Indeed, he made a second attempt which was no more successful than the first.

What is remarkable about the work of Saccheri is the fact that he was the first to prove a great many of the propositions of non-Euclidean geometry, the first man to see what these geometries were like. Though he had discovered a new mathematical continent, he never realized that he had done so. It is for this reason that he is not counted among the discoverers of non-Euclidean geometry. This honor was reserved for Gauss—who, however, published nothing on the subject—for Bolyai, Lobachewsky and Riemann.

The discovery of non-Euclidean geometry was nothing else but a realization supported by adequate proof that Euclid's fifth postulate is independent of his other postulates. But if it is independent, then it can be replaced by any other postulate which is not inconsistent with the remaining postulates. That is the task which the discoverers of non-Euclidean geometry accomplished. Of course, no one man did all of this unaided. Today that task has been completed.

A comparison of the two types of non-Euclidean geometry with that of Euclid may not be out of place here. Consider a straight line drawn in a plane. Take any point of the plane not on the given line. Through this point, one and only one parallel to the given line can be drawn if we accept the postulates of Euclid. If we change his fifth postulate so as to read: *Through a given point, not on a given line, more than one line can be drawn not intersecting the given line,* we obtain the first of the non-Euclidean geometries to be discovered. It is now called hyperbolic geometry. In this geometry the sum of the angles of any triangle is always less than two right angles. To obtain the geometry of Riemann, now called elliptic geometry, we must make two changes in the postulates of Euclid. The implicit assumption of Euclid that all lines are infinite must be replaced by the postulate: *Every straight line is boundless.* Euclid's fifth postulate is replaced by the assumption: *Two straight lines always intersect one another.* In this geometry the sum of the angles of any triangle is always greater than two right angles.

The geometry of a sphere helps to illustrate some of the theorems of elliptic geometry. On a sphere the shortest distance between any two points is the great circle passing through these points. Again any two points on the sphere, if they be not the end points of a diameter, determine one and only one great circle. Hence the great circles on a sphere take the place of straight lines in the Euclidean plane. Now there are no parallel great circles on a sphere since any pair of great circles intersect in two points. It is to be noted that the analogy here is not perfect since the great circles intersect in two points instead of in just one as in elliptic geometry. Again the sum of the angles of any triangle on the sphere is always greater than two right angles.

Do we live in a Euclidean or a non-Euclidean world? We live in a real world, not in a mathematical abstraction. In that real world, which of the abstract geometries applies? We could settle the question if we could verify, for example, whether the sum of the angles in some physical triangle is actually equal to two right angles or is greater than two right angles or less than two right angles. The angles would be measured by instruments, and hence there would always be a certain instrumental error which might be just enough to cover or hide the real difference of the sum from two right angles. We do know that Euclidean geometry is a very good approximation to the geometry of the world in which we live. We do not know, however, whether our world is actually Euclidean. For all practical purposes the theorems of Euclidean geometry apply. This is fortunate, since the theorems of non-Euclidean geometry are not nearly so simple.

The impact of the discovery of non-Euclidean geometries has

been revolutionary in mathematics. Modern mathematicians are very sceptical now of self-evident truths. The more radical among them would subscribe to the statement which appears in a recent text: "No 'self-evident' proposition has ever been found." But then so many of the modern mathematicians, for all their knowledge of logic and mathematics, are notably deficient in philosophical training and background. Nevertheless, the postulational approach to mathematics is now all but universal. All branches of mathematics are now modeled on Euclid. But the postulates are no longer considered as true statements. In fact, they could not possibly be either true or false, since they are statements about undefined symbols. Pure mathematics today abstracts completely from reality. So true is this that Bertrand Russell could define mathematics as the science "in which we never know what we are talking about, nor whether what we are saying is true."

One of the results of the new attitude toward mathematics is the preoccupation with the problem of the consistency of the fundamental assumptions of mathematics. If they were true, there would be no problem of consistency. They would necessarily be consistent. Since their truth cannot be determined, it is of the utmost importance that they be shown to be consistent. At present, this is still one of the unsolved problems of mathematics.

We conclude this study of Euclid with two quotations from mathematicians of note. De Morgan wrote: "There never has been, and till we see it we never shall believe that there can be, a system of geometry worthy of the name, which has any material departures (we do not speak of *corrections* or *extensions* or *developments*) from the plan laid down by Euclid." T. L. Heath has this to say: "Euclid's work will live long after all the textbooks of the present day are superseded and forgotten. It is one of the noblest monuments of antiquity; no mathematician worthy of the name can afford not to know Euclid, the real Euclid as distinct from any revised or rewritten versions which will serve for schoolboys or engineers."

BERNARD A. HAUSMANN

SELECTED BIBLIOGRAPHY

HEATH, T. L., *The Thirteen Books of Euclid's Elements.* Cambridge.
HALSTEAD, G. B., *Girolamo Saccheri's Euclides Vindicatus.* University of Chicago.
HILBERT, D., *The Foundations of Geometry,* authorized translation by E. J. Townsend. University of Chicago.
WOLFE, H. E., *Introduction to Non-Euclidean Geometry.* Dryden.
EUCLID, *Elements of Geometry, Book I.* Regnery.

Aristotle: On Interpretation, *Chapters 1-10*

PHILOSOPHY, unlike natural sciences, does not have the task of discovering something new, of which we have no consciousness whatsoever in our prephilosophical experience. Philosophy does not introduce such beings—the nature and existence of which no one suspected—as the microcosms (disclosed to us by the microscope) or the cosmic rays. True philosophy has no sensational discoveries to offer, which might overthrow our entire prephilosophical conception of the world. It enlarges our knowledge not in the dimension of breadth, but in the dimension of depth and of a higher degree of consciousness. The aim set by philosophy is a new awareness of reality; it consists in a full *prise de conscience* of that which is being vaguely disclosed to the human mind in life, that is, in our immediate unquestioning contact.

As Plato and Aristotle said, "to wonder" about being is at the beginning of all philosophy. Instead of taking the content of a naïve knowledge as something self-evident, philosophy wonders about it and desires to attain a completely new understanding of being. This new understanding is an understanding which is critical, that is, which accepts only that which is either indubitably given or strictly proven, that which univocally reveals its existence. It is an understanding which is systematic, that is, a sober exploration of an object, in which every step is proven, and not an unconscious accumulation of accidentally made observations. It is, finally, an understanding in which the different beings reveal themselves in their specific nature, in which their essential, distinctive marks are grasped and formulated with full precision.

It is the ill fate of philosophy that as soon as a philosopher succeeds in exposing a fundamental truth with convincing clarity, one thinks: this is obvious and there was no need of a philos-

opher in order to know it. This would never happen to a
scientific discovery. Nobody would pretend that the X rays were
always known. So it is that philosophy appears completely superfluous to many people. But the superficiality of this judgment
discloses itself when we realize that philosophical knowledge
aims at an always deeper understanding of being and not at a
mere enlargement of our knowledge.

We shall only be able to appreciate philosophy and its work
if we realize the fundamental role of awakedness in the life of
man. To awake more and more, to emerge from a merely prag-
matic contact with the universe, in which we are satisfied with
a knowledge which enables us to use something and to handle
it in our practical life, is one of the great tasks in human life.
To attain an understanding of the nature of a being, to be
focused on a spiritual possession of it for its own sake, to strive
to dig deeper and deeper into this understanding of beings and
of being as such, is the great enrichment which philosophy alone
can give us.

Because of its dimension of depth, philosophy alone leads our
inquiry beyond the realm of *causae secundae* (secondary causes).
The question of *causa prima* (the first cause) has no place in the
framework of any experimental science; in philosophy, on the
contrary, it is *the* one point toward which every other inquiry
ultimately converges. Philosophy not only leads us to this questioning, it even leads to an answer concerning the *causa prima*
in natural theology—toward God as known by mere human
reason.

In Aristotle, whom St. Thomas and many others of his epoch
called "The Philosopher," the above-mentioned task of philosophy is fulfilled in a remarkable way. The difference between
quality and quantity was obviously, in some way, known to man
before Aristotle, but the philosophical distinction of both as being two different categories was his work. He accomplished a
philosophical *prise de conscience* of this fundamental difference.
The same applies to his elaboration of the four types of causes.
Obviously, the artisans of Athens had in their work some consciousness of efficient causality as well as of a final cause (as when,
for instance, they directed themselves to the end of their work).
It would be nonsensical to pretend that the Pre-Socratics or
Socrates had no consciousness whatsoever of efficient causality or

finality. The great new achievement of Aristotle was the full *prise de conscience* of four different types of causality and a systematical, outspoken distinction of their respective marks.

Aristotle can rightly be called the father of logic, though obviously the laws of logic were respected before him, and the syllogism was used and correctly used before him. But, in the sense in which "discovery" applies in the realm of philosophy, Aristotle did discover the sphere of logic.

The logic of Aristotle is remarkable from different points of view. It is remarkable because a philosophical discovery is the more difficult the more obvious and familiar to us something is. It is a greater and more difficult achievement to acquire perspective toward something which we continuously presuppose and use. The nature of concepts and the logical laws are obviously of this kind. The process of self-consciousness which this discovery implies is a classical case of a philosophical approach, of this philosophical awakening which also leads to an exploration of epistemological problems.

Moreover, the logic of Aristotle is one of the genuine philosophical classics of all time. Rarely has a first exploration of a topic resulted in such a perfect, complete and adequate analysis as has Aristotle's *Organon*.

Finally, no other philosophical work can claim a place similar to that which this part of Aristotelian philosophy still holds today. Notwithstanding the manifold objections raised against Aristotelian philosophy, the Aristotelian logical discoveries still form the main content of any textbook on logic.

It is unbelievable, the exactness with which Aristotle here not only exposes the main decisive facts but analyses the problems in their differentiated ramifications. The *De Interpretatione* is one of the rare examples of an unhampered contact with the object, free from all constructions and premature systematizations. How striking is the discovery of the entity of which truth and falsity can be predicated! After stating that a concept as such can be neither true nor false, Aristotle shows that truth and falsity cannot even be predicated of every sentence. A prayer, for instance, though consisting of sentences, is not true or false; it must be a proposition in order to acquire the capacity of being true or false. Or again, Aristotle is masterly in his analysis of the nature of propositions, the necessity of their containing a

verb, the distinction between a simple and a composite proposition, the fact that to every affirmative proposition there corre-
sponds an opposite denial. And here again, Aristotle makes the
great discovery of the difference between contradictory and contrary propositions, and between distributed and undistributed
terms.

One classic discovery follows another. Do we realize the impact of the insight that of two contradictory propositions one
must be true, and the other false; whereas contraries exclude
only the truth of both propositions, but not the falsity of both?
Again and again we must recall that many things so familiar to
us today were grasped for the first time by Aristotle. The merit
of his discoveries is not diminished because we have grown so
familiar with them.

An especially interesting problem is raised when Aristotle
distinguishes between a mere linguistic unity and a real unity.
To have a real unity it does not suffice to attribute different
predicates to a subject, or one predicate to different subjects. In
predicating "white" of a person, and "man" and "walking," no
real unity is affirmed, but only a linguistic combination of different propositions.

Logic is reputed to be anemic, dry, boring; but for the un-
prejudiced mind, Aristotle's logic is a banquet of opulent philosophical exploration.

Perhaps *De Interpretatione* is even more important as an em-
bodiment of the philosophical method *par excellence* than as
a revelation of admirable discoveries in the field of logic. We
are here confronted with a pattern of *the* true philosophical
content with the given data; we have a prototype of intellectual
intuition. Such intuition is always to be found in the history
of philosophy whenever a real discovery has been made, independently of the epistemology for which a philosopher might
plead, and independently of the method which he claims to use.

DIETRICH VON HILDEBRAND

SELECTED BIBLIOGRAPHY

JAEGER, Werner, *Aristotle: Fundamentals of the History of His Development*. Oxford.
Ross, W. D., *Aristotle*. London: Methuen.
ZELLER, E., *Aristotle and the Earlier Peripatetics*. Longmans, Green.
COPLESTON, Frederick, S. J., *A History of Philosophy* (Vol. I). Newman Bookshop.
ARISTOTLE, *On Interpretation*. Regnery.

Lucian: Selections

THERE IS a certain subtle irony contained in the fact that Lucian of Samosata has been tapped by the directors of the Great Books Foundation for a place of honor among the eminent littérateurs, philosophers and religious thinkers of the Western literary tradition. Lucian come-to-life would surely have taken delight in composing a dialog in which those esteemed figures discussed their present exalted state with the serious students of culture who in these modern times are seeking for a comprehensive picture of the great literature on which our culture has been founded. For Lucian has a monstrous contempt for philosophers, from Aristotle down to the meanest, bedraggled fanatic who peddled his counterfeit wares in the bazaars of Egypt, Greece and Asia Minor. He saw religion as a magnificent hoax; its practitioners, fools; its high priests, arrant hypocrites; its effect, a monstrous delusion; its basis, the all-too-human escapades of a heterogeneous collection of not-so-godlike gods and heroes.

It is very likely that modern readers might have some serious doubts, on purely literary grounds, as to the wisdom of his inclusion in this hallowed company. If the Great Books are important for men of the twentieth century, that value surely lies in the solidity, permanence and influence of their ideas. But Lucian had few ideas and less respect for those who claimed to possess them. He may have provided the fundamental attitude of mind for Swift's *Gulliver's Travels*; he surely has amused and diverted countless readers down through the ages, but (where the world *would* be seriously at a loss) were there no Greek Tragedy, the total loss of Lucian's voluminous works would hardly have wrought catastrophe on modern man's view of the antecedents of his culture. There would seem to be little room for doubt but that Lucian is second-class literature.

In this judgment, I feel sure Lucian would himself agree. He would have been flattered and amused at the company he is keeping nowadays and would have taken immense comfort from the success of what he surely saw as monuments to his own extraordinary cleverness, proliferative imagination and vastly detailed knowledge of the content of ancient Greek Literature. Lucian the satirist was extraordinarily catholic in his choice of subjects for ridicule; he swore allegiance to no philosophic master nor bowed before the shrine of any god; one might almost say that he boasted of holding no principles and hence the stream in which he dipped his sharp and vitriolic pen was as wide (and as shallow) as the manifold pretensions of the pompous mountebank or the infinite variety of human foolishness.

The triumph of his sophistical cleverness is found in the work where he is arraigned by the indignant philosophers whom he had portrayed being sold at auction for a pittance to very unwilling and apprehensive buyers, and ends by persuading the proponents of the art of persuasion that he was doing them a favor by debunking their unworthy followers. Well might he have ended that dialog with a postlude, portraying Aristophanes and himself prostrated in Olympian laughter as the eminent philosophers preened themselves on this latest justification of their unending fame and glory.

Lucian was born around 120 A.D. and lived till the end of the century. There is a tradition that he had been apprenticed to his uncle (a statue maker) at an early age but soon deserted the arts for the profession of a lawyer; at this he was not notably successful, ending up as a writer of speeches for others to deliver. A period of travel provided him with the information about the ways of men and morals, and his rhetorical fluency adapted and developed the matter of his experience; as a kind of itinerant lecturer, he enjoyed a certain success. At the age of forty he formally renounced rhetoric in favor of philosophy, but his study thereof merely provided the subjects for his later ridicule of each and all of the traditional schools of Greek thought. In later life he is said to have become a procurator of a part of Egypt (an appointment by the Emperor Commodus). The date of his death is unknown.

In the course of this varied career he produced eighty-two works, mostly in the form of dialogs, ranging in subject over the whole compass of ancient literature, philosophy and mythology.

An extraordinary power of observation, and the talent for pin-
ning down the foibles and failures of the weak-minded and
malicious fraud, easily turned him to satire. It is here that his
talent lay, and here is his claim to fame. The satiric spirit was
old and hallowed in Greek literature, and for his inspiration
and spirit, Lucian surely goes back to the broad humor and riot-
ous caricature that makes Aristophanes the first of humorists in
time and merit.

For all his contempt for the philosophers, Lucian knew them
well, and the technique of the dialog became, under his pen, at
once a clever imitation and also a monstrous caricature of the
painstaking search for truth with which Socrates (through Plato)
confounded the pretensions of the "successful men" of an earlier
time. But where Plato sought in his discussions to clear the air
of the fuzzy generalizations and half truths with which men
comforted themselves in their complacent "wisdom," Lucian
has no positive contribution to make to philosophic thought.
Like a playful gadfly he punctures pomposity and pretense and
distinctly gives the impression of enjoying the game.

Another element of his humor lies in the incongruity of situation; in his *Dialogs of the Dead* he leads his reader into the
lower regions, there to contemplate the adventures of the gods,
heroes and philosophers of the past. Within a scanty framework
of the traditional stories, his mordant humor betrays the fact
that these exalted personages are, even in Hades, the victims of
the same petty, selfish, hypocritical weaknesses as many a mere
mortal man. The total impression conveyed could well have been
the foundation of the tradition reported by Suidas, that Lucian
was in his old age torn to pieces by dogs as a punishment for his
impiety in ridiculing the gods. These and the *Dialogs of the
Gods* are a collection of imaginary conversations, concocted with
a slender basis of fact from the ancient mythology. Thus we are
given a discussion between Prometheus and Zeus, in which the
former argues cogently for release from his presumably eternal
punishment. Some of the stories will pretend to give the background of later developments of a myth; again we will find a
pair of the gods discussing a future course of action—what turns
out to be the traditional form of a well-known mythological tale.
The atmosphere of cynicism, deceit and hypocrisy throughout
these brief dialogs would hardly generate a great deal of admira-

tion for the gods, and Lucian's defense would merely be that he was portraying heroes and gods as he found them described in Homer and in the other epic cycles of the past. One very significant element of the reader's pleasure in these tales is the implied flattery by the author; the more one knows of ancient stories and myths, the more pointed the humor of his tale.

Here we have the full tale of the choice of the fairest of the goddesses to win the golden apple; with crass ingenuity Venus bribes the rustic Paris with promises of the love of Helen; the selection of Ganymede to be the cup bearer of Zeus is bluntly explained; Mercury, messenger and handyman for all the Olympian gods, complains to his Mother, Maia, of the hard life of drudgery that is his. In this catalog there is scarcely an incident in the mythological career of Mercury that is not the subject of dolorous complaint. The tale of Phaëthon stealing the chariot of the Sun is told when Jupiter is blaming Helios for letting his car be stolen. Mercury, in another short conversation, explains to Apollo how one can distinguish the identical twins, Castor and Pollux, which again gives the occasion for recounting some of their more notable adventures. In a word, one might say that the *Dialogs of the Gods* pretends to be the inside story, the off-the-record (hitherto) account of the origin of the traditional stories that formed the basis of ancient Greek literature.

A relic of Lucian's rhetorical career is found in his *Alexander the Oracle Monger*. Here we have a vitriolic attack (the opposite of the panegyric) on a notorious fakir and mountebank who roamed about selling oracles to whomever he could trick into believing his lies. The man was apparently the epitome of all trickery, perjury, cunning and mendacity, to which he added the utmost boldness and versatility; no lie was too great, no hoax too monstrous, and yet at first meeting one would get the impression he was the kindest and gentlest of men as well as the simplest and least sophisticated.

There follows the tale of Alexander's career of pretentious skullduggery. His greatest cleverness was displayed when he had been caught in his lies; there the master really shone in the full glory of his talents. The infinite ingenuity attributed to Alexander in managing his tricks is a function of Lucian's imagination; nothing is too elaborate, nothing too troublesome, nor anything more successful than the ease with which he gulls his victims. He had prophesied that he would live to be one hundred and fifty years old and then would die of a thunderbolt; actually he contracted some vulgar infection at seventy. To ease his feverish brow, cool water was applied to his head, and then at last it became clear that he was totally bald and had been wearing a wig all his life. His funeral was celebrated with a contest between a collection of impostors each striving for the title of official prophet. Lucian concludes with the claim that this exposé has been merely an attempt to win honor for Epicurus, who (he says) was a good and sincere man, not given to shams and a truly great benefactor of the human race.

The Sale of Creeds is a brief dialog in which Zeus and Hermes conduct an auction of a collection of famous philosophers. Each buyer is privileged to question his prospective slave as to his antecedents, accomplishments and talents. With vicious humor, Lucian has each philosopher retail his teaching and the kind of life he can promise his devoted followers. Pythagoras is rather impressive and is bought for two hundred dollars, but Diogenes is sold to a grudging buyer for five cents. Socrates is, ironically, sold to Dion, the tyrant of Syracuse, for two thousand dollars. Chrysippus argues his prospective owner into dialectical confusion, and the poor man parts with his hard-earned money. A Sceptic goes cheaply for twenty dollars to a master who is going to have a hard time with a slave who suspends judgment on everything, especially as to whether he should work.

For this piece of arrogant boldness, Lucian himself is brought to trial by a group of philosophers, resurrected from the dead for the purpose of avenging their honor. Socrates, gentle in life, opens the scene with a violent diatribe, exhorting all to beat and pummel the culprit. Plato is called upon to identify his friends and to announce the charge—the common anger of all at the abuse that has been heaped upon them. Soon, however, the plausible Lucian begins to win them over to his side, and with gentle cozening he shows them that he has been their true friend and defender. Cleverly he lectures them on patience and philosophic forbearance; he quotes their own words back at them, to the end that he be exonerated from their charges. Finally, Philosophy herself is called to witness in his favor. She is accompanied by her handmaidens, Virtue, Truth, Liberty and Free Speech. The trial repairs to the temple of Athena on the

Acropolis, and when Plato declines to argue (as he had done in life), Diogenes is chosen as their spokesman; and well he might, since he had gone for the cheapest price of all—two obols in the *Sale of Creeds.*

Lucian's disarming defense is to admit the truth of everything he has been accused of, and with a neat twist of the story to show that he has really been a true lover of philosophy—if saddened by the quacks and fakers who pretend to be her devotees and whom alone he has been belaboring. In all his works he has merely been trying to show how these false philosophers bear no resemblance to Lady Philosophy herself. As a result, far from being punished, he ought to be honored for his defense of true philosophy. The fakes that he has exposed are seen to be a collection of beggarly frauds, pretending to philosophic detachment, but eager all the while to cadge and steal all the money they can lay hands on. Pretending disdain for honor and fame, they labor by every deceit to win a meretricious glory. A vote is taken and Truth herself leads the chorus in singing the praises of Lucian, while the philosophers join heartily in his honor. In the final scene the false philosophers gather at the base of the Acropolis, and Lucian with a fishing line angles for some of the more desirable specimens below and reels them in to be presented to the court. Symbolically, the bait is a piece of gold. On inspection, the catch appears so foul that each in turn is tossed from the rocks. In the end, Lucian receives a commission to go about the world rewarding such true philosophers as he finds and branding with a hot iron those whom he perceives to be counterfeit wise men. The closing line avers that they will have need of very few crowns.

The last of the works suggested for discussion is *The Dialogs of the Courtesans.* The pattern is much the same as in the preceding works, in this case the speakers being famous courtesans and lovers in ancient Greece, who confide in one another as to the faults of their successful rivals, the perfidy of their "gentleman" friends, the art of stirring jealousy. At times, abusive love letters of the woman scorned are included. These "ladies" are as unscrupulous in striving to attain their purpose as was Alexander with his oracles, and there is not, either from themselves or from Lucian as author, the slightest hint that there is anything morally reprehensible in their conduct. To that extent this work is a clear picture of the moral degradation of the ancient world.

By far the most interesting of Lucian's works is the *True History*, in which he sets out to parody the gullibility and uncritical writing of some of the ancient historians. He frankly states at the beginning of this story (it purports to be a personal adventure of the author) that everything he is to say will be a lie. He appears insulted that historians relate all sorts of marvels and apparently believe that their lies are undetected. Lucian will therefore tell bigger lies and boast that they are lies, all lies. Then he launches into his tale: a wonderful sea voyage out into the Atlantic that takes him to marvelous islands, raises him up into the sky to visit the moon, plunges him into a war with the inhabitants of the sun, drops him off at the Morning Star and thoroughly investigates the heavenly regions.

Neatly deposited once again on the surface of the sea, he meets with a whale 170 miles long, enters his mouth (ship and all) and dwells there for six months, during which he fights a war with the people who live inside. Bored with this stage of his adventures, he escapes (by means of his amazing ingenuity, which would put the Wily Odysseus in the shade) and pays a visit to the Island of the Blest. There he meets a great many mythological characters, both good and bad, since, while he is there, the wicked who had been in a state of punishment and prison break loose and attack the abode of the Blest. They are repulsed by the defending forces, peace is restored and Lucian and his men set out for home, but (the slyest touch of all!) he has to stop at Calypso's island, to deliver a note from Odysseus wherein she is told that that great hero regrets his staunch fidelity to Penelope, and at the first opportunity he will slip away to spend the remaining days of eternity with her.

These few works then, are a fair sample of the voluminous output of Lucian. While we do not look to him for any profound thoughts or philosophic truth, he still has his place as a sort of lower-case social historian. He has the satirist's sharp eye for the failings of human nature, and it is the triumph of his wit that he applies all of these to the "gods" of antiquity. Basically, he represents the common-sense view, refusing to be taken in by the empty myths that surrounded ancient religion. His greatest weapon is his fertile imagination, joined to his racy humor. His virtues, however, are ephemeral; in refusing to take ancient philosophy and religion seriously, he yet shows his own acquaintance with them, and in passing draws attention to their main tenets; his own contribution, however, is merely that of amusement, and he has nothing to substitute for what he has so amusingly destroyed.

EDWIN A. QUAIN

SELECTED BIBLIOGRAPHY

JEBB, R. C., *Essays and Addresses*. London.
Oxford Classical Dictionary, Art: "Lucian."
LUCIAN, *Dialogs*. Regnery.

St. Thomas: De Magistro

ALCUIN was five centuries dead; St. Albert was in retirement. Yet both Europe's schoolmaster and his own seemed to live and teach again at Paris when St. Thomas wrote his unexcelled treatise *De Magistro (Of the Teacher)*. Because Paris had known many such as Alcuin and St. Albert (and Abélard as well), no trite discussion or trivial defense of the art of teaching could have made these masters live anew for an aggressive university audience of the mid-decade of the greatest of medieval centuries.

By then, the art of teaching was well established, and Paris was its home. In and about the cobbled campus of its great University, teaching had a prestige second only to that of the episcopacy; the century, thirteenth of the Christian era, was as much dedicated to education as would be the nineteenth to material progress. Teachers dominated the times. Never since has the teaching profession attained such social stature; never again would so many seek true culture at so much cost in personal sacrifice. Scholars sought, after many an ardent discussion, a reasoned analysis and definitive pronouncement on the philosophy of teaching from a recognized master. St. Thomas provided them—and an entire Christian tradition—with an answer in one of his biweekly disputations now known as the *De Magistro*.

Although St. Thomas was in his early thirties and had but recently acquired the title of Master in Sacred Theology, he had long been a master of the art of teaching and, among his contemporaries, was the most capable of advancing principles and of answering difficulties upon the ever-controversial subject of education and educators. Much of his own intensive teaching career lay before him, but the theological and philosophical norms of teaching were already solidly in his possession. Principles of metaphysics and psychology governed his every judgment; the practicality of his views was sealed in his own success.

He had already written his basic philosophical work, *On Being and Essence,* and his theological missionary manual, *Against the Gentiles,* was in preparation. Although he had completed a commentary upon the then-standard theological text, the *Sentences* of Peter Lombard, which his own original work was to supplant, St. Thomas meditated for yet another ten years—an interval filled with many other writings—to fit into place all the parts of his masterpiece, the *Summa Theologica.* Even at the time of his composing the *De Magistro,* however, St. Thomas had, in his life and in his writing, the theocentric ground plan which brought sanctity to him and unrivaled superiority to his works. To that ground plan, best formulated in the outline of the *Summa Theologica,* all his other writings must be referred, not indeed for their historical or chronological position, but for their place in his thought.

The thought of St. Thomas was fundamentally theological. Specific problems or philosophical commentaries elicited from him an approach and an emphasis that were truly philosophical, but the horizons of his thought were the full sweep of reality beginning and ending in God as supernaturally revealed. His consistent theological orientation, far from limiting or distorting his thought, actually gave a basic autonomy and ultimate value even to fragments of his works, especially to the *De Magistro.*

In the theological setting of the teacher's relation to God, St. Thomas approached the problems of the art of teaching. For him, the teacher has an almost monarchic role in God's governance of the universe. Infinitely perfect and infinitesimally provident, God has no need for an emissary or intermediate cause in producing effects throughout the universe. Without restraining His power in bringing about the effects His wisdom has predetermined, He has, however, enlisted His creatures in the accomplishment of the cosmic strategies of His Providence. In His infinite goodness He has caused other things to be causes. No less than celestial spheres and irrational elements, the free actions of men have a part, indeed a major part, in the eternal designs of God. Among human actions, that of teaching, because of the spirituality of its content and the spontaneity of its motivation, most perfectly images God.

This concatenation of causes under God in the educative process, explicit in the *Summa Theologica,* remains implicit in the *De Magistro.* Of its four questions, two are devoted to the intrinsic nature of the action of imparting knowledge: whether one man can teach another, or whether God alone can do so, and whether anyone can be called a teacher of himself. The two remaining questions, whether man can be taught by an angel, and whether teaching is a function of the active or contemplative life, deal with the qualifications and motivations of teachers. All four questions succinctly manifest the stature of the educator before God and men. To modern readers the *De Magistro,* with its unquestioned place in Western culture, may not seem startling in its conclusions; it can never fail to be provocative in its principles.

The basic principle of the educative process, and consequently of the theory and practice of the *De Magistro,* is the actualization of potentialities. While this Aristotelico-Thomistic principle of moderate realism has its application to the problem of the eduction of forms in physics, and in ethics to the acquisition of virtue, it has a particularly felicitous role in describing the process of learning. In that process both the potentialities and their actualization are unique. With daring ingenuity and cogent simplicity, St. Thomas used this subtle and intriguing principle of an active potentiality to forge his own distinctive theory of education. According to the predominant antecedent opinions— never quite as primitive as those of modern Gestalt or behavioristic schools—the acquisition of knowledge is either a totally passive reception from an exterior agent or an autonomously active remembrance of innate forms upon the occasion of sense stimulation. Excluding both extremes, St. Thomas employed the Aristotelian principle of an active potentiality as a middle course, not of compromise but of strict conformity to reality.

Agreeing in reasonable measure with Platonic immanence, St. Thomas observed that

there preexist in us certain potentialities of knowledge; namely, the first concepts of the intellect which are recognized immediately by the light of the active intellect through the species abstracted from sense presentation, whether the concepts are complex as axioms or simple as an idea of being, unity, or something of this nature which the intellect grasps immediately.

Obviously opposed to any Platonic interpretation, however, is St. Thomas's insistence that even those germinal capacities are the resultants of sense experience denuded of individualizing characteristics by the active intellect of the person who employs them in further learning. On the other hand, while recognizing the contribution of objective reality, St. Thomas rejected Avicenna's interpretation of Aristotle's attributing knowledge to infusions from a separate agent. For him,

when something exists in active, complete potentiality the extrinsic agent acts only by helping the intrinsic agent by ministering to it those things by means of which it comes forth into actuality, just as a doctor in healing is a minister to nature, which does the principal work. . . . Knowledge, therefore, preexists in the learner not in purely passive potentiality, but in active potentiality.

Granted this active potentiality, God's endowment of the educable, and the first step in education, a man may either approach the unknown through discovery, autonomously applying self-evident principles to new problems, or he may appeal to a teacher. In the latter case,

the teacher proposes to another by means of symbols the discursive process which he himself goes through by natural reason, and thus the natural reason of the student comes to a cognition of the unknown through the aid of what is proposed to him as with the aid of instruments . . . and this is teaching.

Education, then, is an imitation as well as an implementation of nature in the learning process. The teacher's proposal of his own discursive process, moreover, does not devitalize the student's intellectual activity, but rather fortifies it. The student himself must actively parallel the thought pattern of the teacher, so that the two may be of one mind, similar in their sharing of truth. Instrumental in linking the thoughts of the teacher with those of the student are the symbols of reality which the teacher employs. Rough-hewn in reality, the intelligibility in things takes on a new condition in symbols. It is no less effective in its contribution to knowledge, since

the words of the teacher, heard or seen in writing, have the same relation to causing knowledge in the intellect as anything outside the mind, because from both the intellect takes the intelligible content. In fact, while their inner meaning is preserved, the symbolic presentation of realities, as stripped of individualizing characteristics and as more proximately intelligible, actually facilitates the learning process. Symbols substitute for the perceptibles in the teacher's ministrations to the learner, but neither the symbols nor the teacher supplant reality or the learner's self-activity, which is always immanent but never independent.

The dependence upon the teacher of the learner, as distinguished from the discoverer, is the subject of the second point of inquiry in the *De Magistro:* whether a man can teach himself. Applying the common principle that a "thing acts according as it is actual," St. Thomas briefly points out that teaching implies "the perfect action of knowledge in the teacher," whereas in the learner only an intellectual plasticity and interested cooperation are presupposed. This initial superiority of the teacher is his warranty to existence—and incidentally is that of the Great Books. While neither can be compared to a human mind actually discovering truth, both the great books and "the teacher who has the knowledge of the whole explicitly can lead to knowledge more quickly and easily than anyone can be led by himself."

The learner and the teacher, then, are coefficients in the same act; the learner supplies vital receptivity, and the teacher a mediative perfection in knowledge. Being self-active in learning is not the same as being self-taught. The latter, commendable as it is—though not to the degree of Schopenhauer's exaggerations—is always laborious and frequently unproductive. A self-active discipleship is no less industrious, especially as it results in a wider contact with human experience when it shares in the intellectual perfections of either great books or great teachers.

The greatness of the teacher, and consequently of his written instruments, is measured by his possession and presentation of truth as compared with the work of others in the same field. The hierarchy of teachers who possess and present truth includes not only God and men, but angels as well, a proposition which concludes the third inquiry in the *De Magistro.* More than a merely quaint medieval digression, the solution to the problem of angelic teaching establishes many of the norms for appraising the relative merits of all teachers.

Beyond rivalry is God's teaching, so radical that it presupposes nothing in the learner, "because He endows the mind itself with the intellectual light and impresses on it the knowledge of first principles." Human efforts are more humble, however; they are limited to bringing to actuality what is implicitly and potentially contained in principles already possessed by the learner. Between these two is the angelic manner of teaching men. The angel cannot give man an intellect, but he can fortify it. He cannot exercise the divine prerogative of infusing ideas, but—even without the use of exterior symbols—he can mingle phantasms in the imagination to occasion new trends of thought. While no human teacher can equal such angelic action, the more closely he approximates it by the superiority of his grasp of his subject and the clarity and cogency of his presentation, the more he will appear as great among his colleagues. His scholarship will give him authority and his personality will have an added inspirational value, but at best he will remain human and limited, a master who ministers.

The ministrations of teachers have a profound social significance, of which St. Thomas took careful note in his response to the fourth inquiry of the De Magistro. Since all human life, as intellectual and volitional activity, is either contemplative or active, merchants and lawyers, mechanics and laborers, and above all educators, live in either of these ways according to the content and motivation of their intellectual lives. Although it is not common in offices or factories, the contemplative life is not restricted to the cloister. Wherever its object and end are realized, it exists. Its object, "the knowable reasons for things," is even separable from its end, "the consideration of truth."

The active life, on the other hand, has as its object "the temporal things with which human life deals," and as its aim "the utility of one's neighbor." That utility, the social benefit of what has already been learned, is the motive force in teaching—as opposed, for example, to the scholarly pursuit of personal intellectual perfection. Yet, teaching takes its object from the contemplative life rather than the active, and thus combines the two. It rises above the day-to-day occurrences of individual human lives to attain the "knowable reasons for things," but with these reasons it returns to the analysis and answering of basic human problems in the interest of society. If the social stature of teaching has become degraded since the writing of the *De Magistro,* it is probably because educators themselves have either neglected their social obligations or have failed to find the reasons for things. In either case they have neither applied the principles nor followed the evident practice of the *De Magistro.*

St. Thomas exemplified each of his educational principles within the brief scope of the *De Magistro.* As much aware as Herbart or Dewey that self-activity in learning depends upon interest and a problem, St. Thomas engrossed his audience by presenting first the objections to his own point of view in a form often more trenchant than that of their original propo-nents. To these apparently devastating arguments, he then op-posed authoritative statements of Scripture, the Fathers, or philosophers, whose probative value rebuffed but did not quell a questioning intellect. The intellectual satisfaction which dis-pelled all doubt came only with his reasoned analysis of the subject at hand. Succinctly and cogently stated, each argument included both the basic principles and apposite illustrations necessary to reach a logical and convincing conclusion. Finally, exposing half truths and sophistries, St. Thomas painstakingly answered each of the objections by applying again the principles of his own positive argument. This procedure demanded a maximum of self-activity and yet never neglected the initial plasticity of the learner.

If, for modern readers, the inspiring personality of St. Thomas is not always apparent in his teaching method, it is none the less present. As a teacher, he was not the object of inquiry but a means of knowledge. Not a study in himself, he was, in reality, what Emerson imagined to be the "transparent eye of nature." The objectivity of his lucid presentation of the "knowable reasons for things" he had contemplated has given some the altogether false impression of a frigid, monkish erudition, in-different to human needs. Quite the contrary is true. In teaching and in writing, as the *De Magistro* bears eloquent witness, he sought to share with all, those theological and philosophical principles which would contribute most to the utility of his neighbor.

Any appraisal of the *De Magistro* in the light of the "big, booming, buzzing confusion" of modern educational theory would immediately expose it to ridicule. Considered in the context of our contemporary naturalistic atmosphere of education, St. Thomas's principles are "out of due time." Educators subscribing to naturalism—in which, as William James observed, "ideals appear as inert by-products of physiology; what is greater is explained by what is lower"—could not tolerate St. Thomas as a colleague. For them, statistics are the criteria of science, and tenuous generalizations the source of their admittedly dubious conclusions. But of one thing they seem certain—nature, "the sum of things and events in space and time, subject to a single system of casual laws," has supplanted the supernatural, the Christian concept of God's providential care. Excluded, with the supernatural, is St. Thomas's description of the teacher's cooperation in an eternal design.

Judged by Christian standards, however, which are no less scientific for admitting the supernatural, the *De Magistro* appears as the most perfect single document of its kind. Its estimate and expectations of human nature are as thoroughly Christian as is its theocentric approach. The problems it entertains and the solution it offers are marked with the principles and method of the Master Himself. Uncongenial as it is to the secular mind, it has nevertheless a tremendous fecundity as a manual of educational procedure and principles. The greatness of the *De Magistro*, then, is the mustard-seed magnificence of Christianity itself.

DOMINIC HUGHES, O.P.

SELECTED BIBLIOGRAPHY

St. THOMAS AQUINAS, *Summa Theologica*, Prima Pars, q. 117. Benziger.
POPE PIUS XI, *The Christian Education of Youth*, 1923.
SLAVIN, Robert J., "The Thomistic Concept of Education," *Essays in Thomism*. Sheed & Ward.
MAYER, M. H., *The Philosophy of Teaching of St. Thomas Aquinas* (includes translation of *De Magistro* into English). Bruce.
O'CONNELL, Geoffrey, *Naturalism in American Education*. Benziger.
BRUBACHER, John S., *Modern Philosophies of Education*. McGraw-Hill.
St. THOMAS AQUINAS, *De Magistro*. Regnery.

Song of the Volsungs and the Nibelungs

After the death of Brynhild there were two bale-fires made, one for Sigurd, and that burned first, and on the other was Brynhild burned, and she was on a chariot which was decked with rich hangings. Thus it is told that Brynhild fared in the chariot on Hel-way. . . .

From *The Hell-Ride of Brynhild*

THE TREE OF STORY grew first in Paradise, where also sprang up the clear spring that later, in India, became the Ocean of Story. In Greece the witch Medea brought some of that original water to a boil as she stirred in Myth and History. In Bagdad, Scheherazade watched her damascened Cauldron simmer for the Caliph, who liked Story passing well when he wasn't fighting against the great-limbed warriors from the barbaric land good Moslems called Frangistan, after the men of the Franks, and which his Persian allies named Varangistan, instead, after the golden-haired Varangians who came in dragon-ships to guard the Greek Emperor in his palace at Byzantium. The Pot of Story would soon bubble up again in those same Frankish lands of the West, with the matter of Britain as told by those great Frangistani, Geoffrey of Monmouth and Chrétien de Troyes and Marie de France. It was, within a century after that, due to overflow in the wild Varangian lands as well; and there the Pot of Story would take on the mile-wide dimensions of the famous mead-kettle that the god Thor stole for the Aesir from giant Hrymer.

For the thirteenth century was destined to be, among so many other good things, the age of the saga-men, who gave to Europe one of its two medieval bodies of epic prose, the other corpus being the Irish hero-tale, which had, in the days when Olaf the White ruled in Dublin, powerfully influenced the beginnings of saga.

As a matter of fact, the *Volsungasaga* is not a particularly resplendent example of the saga form. On its own merits it cannot stand with *Laxdaela* or *Gisli* or *Njál*. It represents, in one sense, the escapist end of a long and vital narrative tradition. It stands to the first sagas almost as the historical romances of Bulwer-Lytton to the sturdy excellences of *Tom Jones;* or, to employ what is probably a fairer analogy, it stands to the greater family sagas as does the stirring action of Scott's *Ivanhoe* to the more authentic values of the same author's *Heart of Midlothian.*

Nevertheless, despite this relative technical decadence, modern readers have reason to prize the *Volsungasaga* very highly. It is our most direct road to what William Morris once called "the Great Story of the North which should be to all our race what the Tale of Troy was to the Greeks." It must rank with the high companies of Troy and Camelot as one of the three master-stories of the Western World. And it makes us free of the northern lights that play so baleful cold and burning clear over the ancient Eddic poems, of which the *Volsungasaga* is a late redaction. Through it, we gain easy acquaintance with the twin essences of old Norse literature: poetry so piercing sharp it quivers to its twanging goal like a Viking arrow; prose so sheerly and magnificently prosaic it almost fells the reader, as with the blunt edge of a Viking war-ax. (In this latter connection, incidentally, it should be pointed out that the Morris translation is extremely good; but so deliberately archaist that the contemporary reader, who does not know the Old Icelandic original, can get no fair impression of the startling modernity—almost Hemingwayesque—of saga diction and stylistics.)

The *Volsungasaga* got itself written down in Iceland sometime toward the end of the thirteenth century very near the date, as a matter of fact, when, in Austria, the other great Sigurd compilation, the medieval High German *Nibelungenlied,* was also being composed. The events it narrates are, however, much older than the thirteenth century. They belong to the heroic age of *Germania;* they are our bequest from the non-Roman pre-Christian North. The ancient heroes are Frankish; the even more ancient gods are Norse. The story of Sigurd grew up first among the Rhenish Franks and was most probably carried from northwestern Germany into Norway sometime in the seventh century, along with the coins of Charlemagne that have been dug up in Viking barrows.

In Norway it underwent a sea-change into something both starker and richer than what had been before in South Germany; for the world of the *Eddas* is both a grimmer and a greater world than the world of the somewhat romanticized *Nibelungenlied*. Siegfried became Sigurd, and Kriemhild, Gudrun. Brynhild was transformed into a Valkyrie. Burgundian Gundicarius emerged as Gunnar. Hunnish Attila found himself the dread Atli who, in story, fell under the triple Volsung doom. But the gods were already in residence there in the northland: Odin and Loki and Thor—and the Norn sisters who sit behind the gods under the shadow of Wyrd, That Which Is Becoming. When it came to fate, Varangistan had always lowered even darker than Frangistan.

We do not know the name of the redactor who collected and arranged the Volsung stories in the *Volsungasaga*. His work is basically a prose paraphrase of the far more intense Sigurd, Gudrun and Brynhild ballads in the poetic *Edda*. His Sigurd is drawn, in part, from the *Thridreksaga;* and he may also have used an earlier *Sigurthsaga* which was later lost. As a result of these varied origins, the *Volsungasaga* is a thing of faulty proportions. There is about it an overplus of savage and somber grandeur. The house of Atreus had a doom upon it. Here are dooms laid on three houses: the Volsungs; the Giukings or Nibelungs; the swart Budlung house of Hunnish Atli. And the dooms work themselves out within so short a compass that it is as if Aeschylus had piled all the toppling events of his Agamemnonian trilogy into a single play.

The *Volsungasaga* is the fierce avatar of that elusive essence we call, purely for the sake of convenience, the romantic. But, though romantic, it is not of Rome. The culture of western man had four strong roots. It derives its soul from Judea; its mind from Greece; its will from Rome; and, last in time but not least in impact, its imagination from Norse and Celtic pagandom. Rome, it is true, baptized this new imagination; house-broke, as it were, the jewelled unicorns who draw the golden cart wherein lie the sleeping archetypes of Story.

But a new wind was blowing over the spirit of man all during the dark and early Middle Ages—a wind from the Well at the World's End that lies somewhere east o' the sun and west o' the moon; a wind from the beginnings of the world; a springtide wind from off the Northern nesses, the "beakéd promontory" of Milton's great image, where is the "haunt of seals and orcs, and sea-mews' clang"; a wind from out the Druid forests of Britain and Ireland. Here, at last, instinct with young barbarian vigor, was a new thing under the sun; a thing so vital that the weary Latin sentences could not cope with it. They broke beneath the new magic; and new vernaculars came into being to bear the weight of the fresh, new insights.

One is always, of course, at liberty to reject the barbarian bequest; to mourn the vanished balance of classic decorum; even to insist—which is true enough—that this "new thing" was not so utterly new but that more than once it had looked out at the ancient world from under the brows of Circe and Polyphemus. Dante Gabriel Rossetti, speaking once to William Morris, summed up the rational Mediterranean case against the whole Dark Age complex of Morris and Wagner by saying that "it was absolutely impossible for him to feel any interest at all in anyone whose brother was a dragon." As a matter of fact, on this particular subject of Wagner's treatment of the Nibelung tale, Morris agreed with Rossetti. His daughter, May Morris, has left an amusing account of how her leonine father used to mock the stertorous Wagnerian heroics, especially that moment when tenor Siegfried, finding Brynhild sleeping on the mountain, surprisedly carols the anticlimactic line: *Das ist kein Mann.* As for Regin, Sigurd's foster-father whose brother was the dragon Fafnir, Rossetti might have inveighed with equal justice against that other member of this hybrid family who was an otter and who hobnobbed familiarly with a gold-hoarding dwarf named Andvari who, in *his* protean turn, swam about in the shape of a pike.

But, in the last analysis, Rossetti's pre-Raphaelite scorn of what Morris truly called the "monstrous order" of the *Volsungasaga* is a rather serious esthetic limitation. Oxford's Professor Tolkien, amateur of dragons and fast friend of Clive Staples Lewis, knows a good deal more about following the hot spoor of the lingworm:

I never imagined that the dragon was of the same order as the horse. And that was not solely because I saw horses daily, but never even the footprint of a worm. The dragon had the trade-mark *Of Faërie* written plain upon him. In whatever world he had his being, it was an Other-World. Fantasy, the making or glimpsing of Other-Worlds, was the heart of the desire of Faërie. I desired dragons with a profound desire. Of course, I in my timid body did not wish to have them in the neighbourhood, intruding into my relatively safe world, in which it was, for instance, possible to read stories in peace of mind, free from fear. But the world that contained even the imagination of Fafnir was richer and more beautiful, at whatever cost of peril. The dweller in the quiet and fertile plains may hear of the tormented hills and the unharvested sea and long for them in his heart. For the heart is hard though the body be soft. ("On Fairy Tales," p. 63, *Essays Presented to Charles Williams*, Oxford.)

One cannot deny that Fafnir is a creature of Faërie; that he belongs to the bestiary of legend and not to Buffon or Cuvier. But he is also the most realistic and least fantastic of dragons. His loathsome length, so like the veritable saurians of the *Ur-slime* and so unlike the glossy extravagances of Renaissance Spenser and Ariosto, is a fitting heraldic emblem for the Northern thing in literature. The Mediterranean world of Vergil and Catullus had little to learn of *lacrimae rerum;* and the Rome of Horace knew far more of *nugae rerum* than the Varangian lands were ever to know, at least until the far-off day of Hans Andersen's golden *chinoiseries.* But, with *Germania,* the dark shadows of *tenebrae rerum* sink deep into the European consciousness: the hideous barrow dwellers of the sagas; Grendel and his awful dam haunting the misty heath; Volsung Sigmund and Sinfjotli putting on the wolf skins in the musty earth-house; the vengeances of Brynhild and of Gudrun. There were, it is true, such *femmes fatales* as Medea and Clytemnestra before the shield-maiden whom Sigurd loved and the daughter of Budli whom he married. But those Northern queens remain the archetypal *femmes fatales* all the same. From their lethal haughtiness stem the desperate ballad heroines of Scotland and Denmark; Ibsen's Hedda Gabler; Erlend Nikalausson's leman, Eline Ormsdatter, before he married Kristin Lavransdatter; *Wuthering Heights's* pitiful Cathy, who would not rest in the quiet earth amid the Yorkshire heath and harebells and the sheep grazing on the moors.

Cathy was even more like the tragic Brynhild of the Eddic poems, she who was stopped by the giantess as she rode down Hell causeway on her way to join Sigurd after they both rose in death from the bale-fires kindled for them. The giantess taunts her with being both murderess and adulteress, and, in reply, Brynhild affirms her innocence, blames fate, and bids the troll-wife let her pass, for she and her hero shall live out eternity together:

> Yet Gudrun reproached me   Giuki's daughter,
> That I in Sigurd's   arms had slept;
> Then did I hear   what I would were hid,
> That they had betrayed me   in taking a mate.
>
> Ever with grief   and all too long
> Are men and women   born in the world;
> But yet we shall live   our lives together,
> Sigurd and I.   Sink down,   giantess!

The poet of the *Edda* is much more merciful to Brynhild than is the compiler of the *Volsungasaga*. In the *Short Lay of Sigurd* he absolves her utterly of blame, adding: *It was the Fates that worked them ill.* This indictment of the *grimmar Urdir* is fairly uncommon in the sagas. Far more even than in Greek tragedy, Fate there ruled supreme. The Northern mind could not fathom the Sophoclean subtlety, expressed in *Oedipus Tyrannos,* of Fate and free will intersecting in the plane of time and space in such a way that free will, without destroying itself, became the hand-maiden of destiny. The saga-men knew that each one "maun dree his weird." Brynhild knew beforehand it was fated to come to pass that the three great houses would go down in blood and flame because of her unrequited love for Sigurd; and even so did she tell Gudrun, the princess who was to be her rival:

". . . for Sigurd shall come to thee, even he whom I have chosen for my well-beloved; and Grimhild shall give him mead mingled with hurtful things, which shall cast us all into mighty strife. Him shalt thou have, and him shalt thou quickly miss; and Atli the king shalt thou wed; and thy brethren shalt thou lose, and slay Atli withal in the end."

Gudrun answers, "Grief and woe to know that such things shall be!"

And therewith she and hers get them gone home to King Giuki.

Sigurd of the Volsungs was the greatest man in the North. Yet he did not withstand the blow of Guttorm, brother of Gun-nar and Hogni and his youngest brother-in-law, he who incurred no blood-guilt because he stood "clean out of all the oaths moreover." For Sigurd "might not deal with his shapen fate, nor the measure of his life-days."

Something magnificent, it must be admitted, emerges from this fatalistic Northern attitude toward *la condition humaine;* and something sinister as well. In its excesses, in its ultimate denial of *hubris,* it moves toward the political buffoonery of the Nietzschean *Uebermensch.* In its highest manifestation it gives us a Hero *par excellence* who is unfellowed in his dying and intolerable when he wins; who is, in other words, the finest of ballad themes and the most ruinous of political leaders. The Northern Hero rides out of the Varangian forests and into our consciousness as surely as, before him, the Citizen, toga flung negligently across one shoulder, strolled from out the Roman *urbs.* The Citizen is a more valuable concept, certainly, than the Hero; but he is not nearly so exciting. He is not an archetype. He is not man alone, man against the universe; pre-Christian, pre-Roman man. And something heady and unregenerate in us makes us prefer the Hero to the Citizen-Philosopher. The Hero's is the quality that, flashing out of the Viking darkness into the breast of Renaissance Hamlet, allows Horatio's sweet Prince to send Rosencrantz and Guildenstern to their deaths, "not shriving time allowed," and makes him warn Laertes: "Yet have I something in me dangerous, which let thy wiseness fear." One-eyed All-Father Odin puts it best of all in *Havamal:*

> The son of a king   shall be silent and wise,
>   And bold in battle as well;
> Bravely and gladly   a man shall go,
>   Till the day of his death is come.

> The sluggard believes   he shall live forever,
>   If the fight he faces not;
> But old age grants him   no meed of quarter
>   Though spears may for a time.

It is the Hero's uncomplicated, all-sufficient code. As the shield-wall bends at Maldon and the grey spears rain ever more heavily on the survivors, Thought is but "the harder, Heart the keener, Mood the more, as our Might lessens." Sigurd at bay before the Giukings, Thormod killing his enemies in the cave mouth, Njál sending out arrows from the loft, Colonel Richard Cantwell, broken nose "like a gladiator's in the oldest statues," musing on the *mystique* of soldiery in Hemingway's latest novel and finding it "the oldest and best of trades, although most people who practice it are unworthy"—it is all down here in the laconic starkness of the *Volsungasaga;* and down here first— for Homer's *Iliad,* greater masterpiece that it is, lacked the romantic dimension that the modern world, for better or worse, still prizes.

Yet it is not this element alone which has survived in later literature. There is also that unanalyzable quality of Story *as* Story which persists in English letters far and away above all others; in Stevenson and Doyle and Morris and Kipling and C. S. Lewis. Allied with this quintessential narrative essence is an accompanying glow-worm lambency, a green fox-fire for which *atmosphere* is far too pallid a word, and which goes with saga, ballad and the prose of high adventure. Except for Scott and Hardy and the broiling hell fire of *Moby Dick,* in English letters it exists in minor key. It can be found, for example, in Buchan and Walpole, but not in Dickens or Trollope. The Scandinavian novels of Sigrid Undset, Selma Lagerlöf and Verner af Heidenstam are its proper habitat. Probably the greatest critic of medieval literature who ever wrote in the English tongue was Chesterton's old professor at the University of London, W. P. Ker. He called this not-to-be-defined, magical thing from the North "the passage of mystery, the musical close, in which the tragic idea is changed into something less distinct than tragedy, yet without detriment to the main action."

Less distinct than tragedy, surely. But—dare one hint it?— something greater, perhaps. For tragedy is man's reconciliation to fate; and this elusive chiming, whatever else it is, somehow sounds a far-off chord of a more primary reconciliation. For all the turbulence and passion and dark evil that besets the doomed houses, Brynhild strikes a note of otherness in the Eddic original: *Sorrow is the portion of the life of all men and women born; now we two, I and Sigurd, shall be parted no more for ever.* The novel is the human comedy; the drama the human tragedy. Fairy tale, ballad and saga all sight, above the sword-play and the dying, the human hope as well.

The mighty Volsung tree out of which Sigmund drew Odin's magic sword has taproots going down as far into the dark recesses of human nature as world-ash Yggdrasil itself, whose third root stood in heaven. It is watered by blood and terror, by murder and treachery and incest. But its branches are glorious. They have flowered into the music of Wagner, the novel of Undset, the poetry of Coleridge, and the drama of Ibsen.

CHARLES A. BRADY

SELECTED BIBLIOGRAPHY

BELLOWS, Henry A., *The Poetic Edda*. Princeton.
KER, W. P., *Epic and Romance. Essays on Medieval Literature*. Macmillan.
KOHT, Halvdan, *The Old Norse Sagas*. Princeton.
PHILLPOTTS, Bertha S., *Edda and Saga*. Butterworth.
SCHLAUCH, Margaret, *Romance in Iceland*. Allen and Unwin.
Fall of the Nibelungs. Dutton (Everyman's Library).
Song of the Volsungs and the Nibelungs. Regnery.

Calvin: Institutes of the Christian Religion, *Selections*

THE SIXTEENTH CENTURY was a time of ferment. Nationalism, introduced two centuries earlier by Philip the Fair, had finally swept over all Europe. The Western Schism had shaken the spontaneous respect and implicit confidence that Christendom had in the Pope, and as a result, the local princes or the oligarchical bourgeois governments arrogated to themselves greater authority, which they were anxious to increase still more. Latin and Greek learning offered new values to the soul of Western Europe, and the Classical Way of Life, so different from the ascetical and antiworldly axiology of the preceding era, was appealing and was in part accepted. The churchmen still clung to the old framework of ecclesiastical and civil institutions, but they themselves were deeply infected with nationalistic ambitions and, above all, with classical worldliness.

The result was that the churchmen used the ecclesiastical structure as an instrument for other ends. The piety of the people, languidly surviving in spite of a great relaxation of customs, did not take kindly to the profanation of the sacred, but they were helpless to do anything about it. There were cries for reform in all quarters, but there was no plan and not enough energy to bring it about.

Into this highly explosive moment there was thrust a man who was formed by the new Nationalism and the New Learning. His own neurotic temper made a life of piety in terms of ascetical self-conquest very painful. He therefore proposed a vision of Christendom where asceticism would disappear in favor of spontaneity; where philology would take the place of theology; where Nationalism would be a substitute for a united Christendom.

This man was Martin Luther. He is an intriguing figure, nor

did his neurosis wipe out a winsome personality. He was of a brusque, violent nature, but honest, sincere and kindly. He had deep and rich insights, but his intellect was always subservient to psychic pressures which made existence for him an intense anxiety. His new Christianity appealed to the princes and his castigation of the worldliness of the leaders of Christendom pleased the people. Yet Luther did not think that he was producing something new: he believed that he was preaching the true Christian message, which had become obscured by the evil in men. Hence he was surprised and passionately irritated when Christendom did not agree with him, but he stubbornly clung to his ideas and spread them over the German lands.

Luther never made a complete and coherent scheme of his thought. His collaborator, Philip Melanchthon, did this for him. However, there was a young Frenchman who had been strongly influenced by the Lutheran message, and while Melanchthon was slowly making his system, Jean Cauvin, or John Calvin, still in his twenties, built up a Reform theology on principles derived from Luther, though he did not agree with all of Luther's positions. The Calvin work, the justly famous *Institutes of the Christian Religion,* had a great advantage over the work of the other Reformers. As he himself says, he was by nature drawn to brevity and simplicity, and though he does not say it, his work shows he had a systematic and orderly mind.

Calvin had not the impetuous sweep of vision that Luther had. Nor did he have the flashes of brilliant intuition that marked the bedeviled German, but he could weed out the incoherencies of Lutheran thought, and he could build the various elements into a system which was presented as being deliberately different from the theology common to the theologians of his time. Luther, in the beginning of his work, thought the Papacy would take over his theology, but Calvin, from the outset, wanted no approbation of the Pope, and he made him an adversary without a previous papal attack. Calvin was outside the Catholic Church and he wanted to be so, while Luther valiantly accepted a similar situation with no joy and not by design. Calvin was more of a heretic than Luther—but strangely enough, less heretical. He could not get new ideas, though he could combine the new ideas of others with old accepted ones so as to produce a novel amalgam. From that remarkable *complexus oppositorum,* Catholic dogma, Calvin extracted enough pieces to round out a Lutheran core of notions into a reasonable whole.

It is a strange jest of history that the followers of Calvin in the twentieth century will not be able to understand what he is talking about, while the Catholics against whom he railed can still comprehend the burden of his message. The Calvinist approach to Christianity has long since been relinquished by Protestants, and his preoccupations have been silently and reverently relegated to the archive department of the Hall of Fame. There is so much Catholicism in the *Institutes* that the modern Protestant, removed by centuries of separation from Catholic life, simply finds Calvin dealing with problems which for the modern Calvinist have no meaning and no sense.

The two selections of the *Institutes* offered in the Great Books Foundation series (Book II, chap. 2; Book IV, chap. 20) deal with two ideas that are considered distinctive contributions of Calvin to the history of thought and culture. One selection reproduces his doctrine on the total depravity of man since the Fall, and the other reprints Calvin's theory of civil society. It is unfortunate that Calvin's ideas on Predestination are not presented, or his vision of the Church. However, the doctrines offered show Calvin to advantage.

The Calvinistic idea of the total depravity of man is usually considered embarrassing to those who hold it. One recalls the famous story of a pious adherent to Calvinism who, when asked if she really believed in the utter depravity of human beings, answered with a sigh that it was a saving doctrine if one could live up to it. That is, of course, the difficulty in the doctrine; no one can live "up" to it. However, on this point Calvin was by no means so extreme as is popularly believed. His presentation of the doctrine manifests the theological method he followed in everything. By initial commitment he wished to limit his sources of doctrine to the Scriptures, because he accepted enthusiastically the Lutheran idea that only the Bible could give us religious truth. By personal antipathy he was opposed to the Schoolmen, with all their works and pomps. By a natural predilection he favored St. Augustine, whose theology was the chief source of both Luther and Calvin.

These three dynamisms produced a peculiar product. The negations implied by Calvin's first principles did not negate sufficiently. To hate the Schoolmen and to attack them, one has to be a Schoolman, and Calvin was an excellent Scholastic theologian, using the Scholastic method but proceeding from a different set of postulates. Hence, when he dealt with the Scriptures, which he knew very well, he could not deal with them in their pure state. He dealt with scriptural problems as they were developed and discussed *in his time*. His dislike for the Aristotelianism current in the theological schools of his day pushed him into Augustinian thought, which was for him more vital and more illuminating. In the *Institutes,* 180 passages of Augustine are cited, all of them with respect, most of them as expressions of Calvin's views, very few of them to be refuted. Peter Lombard and Thomas Aquinas are quoted on occasion, but they are petulantly dismissed as mistaken or irrelevant. But St. Bernard, a stout Augustinian, is abundantly reproduced and almost always with praise and veneration.

Calvin did not derive his doctrine of man's depravity from the Scriptures. He found it in St. Augustine, whose doctrine he did not understand. Nor did he formulate Augustinianism from an exclusive study of the Augustinian writings, but rather in the light of the Scholastic discussions that surrounded the Augustinian theory. When Calvin is finished with his exposition of the theory of utter depravity, we have not advanced one inch on the Scholastic doctrine on the same subject, but rather regressed hopelessly. We are given the strong words that St. Augustine used in place of the carefully studied phrases that the medieval theologians employed to express the truth in Augustine's teaching. Calvin reproduces more faithfully Augustine's urgency and rhetorical vigor, but as far as the idea itself is concerned, he is inferior to the Scholastics—whose thought he has largely taken over but whose sobriety he condemns.

To put things quite baldly, Calvin never taught the total depravity of human nature. Neither did St. Paul. Neither did St. Augustine. Neither did St. Thomas. Calvin taught what the others had taught, namely, that human nature of itself is incapable of supernatural acts, a truth that is evident on the mere analysis of the terms. There is an added notion, taught by the Schoolmen long before Calvin appeared on the scene, namely, that the unaided human will cannot fulfill adequately the commandments of God. Calvin would have been horror-struck at the modern

Freudian doctrine that teaches that every human act is directed unconsciously to irrational egoistical ends, so that the seeming autonomy of the act is so much self-deception. This is nearer to a theory of total depravity, but Calvin would have fumed if it had reached his ears.

In the question of the freedom of the will, so far from denying it, Calvin insisted that the will was free in everything it does, for otherwise God could not punish it, and Calvin was very anxious that God punish evildoing. He makes it very clear that in the question of man's conduct, we must avoid two extremes; one being the denial of man's responsibility for his actions, and the other the affirmation of man's capacity for Christian righteousness by his own natural endowment rather than by divine grace freely given.

If this is true, why has everyone for so many centuries proposed Calvin as the enemy of free will? Because Calvin himself insisted that he was opposed to the teaching of the Scholastics on this point, when as a matter of fact a calm reading of the content rather than the rhetoric of his thought shows that he was not opposed at all. The Schoolmen, who did not like him, were willing to take him at his word, without reflecting long enough to see that they were using a set language in one way and he was using the same language in another way. Under these circumstances, misinterpretation was inevitable.

In his exposition of the natural powers of man in the present state of things, Calvin admits that man can discover apt ways of doing things needed for our earthly life, and he also admits that new discoveries in this field can be made. Calvin admits that man can know the larger truths entailed in human existence, such as God, morality and religion, but he insists that such knowledge is generally confused and poor. It is hardly the task of a genius to see this truth. The youngest thinker need only look about him and he will realize only too painfully how true it is.

As far as freedom of choice is concerned, Calvin disdainfully concedes it as an irrelevant fact. He only insists that where grace does not enter into an act of choice between different possibilities, the result will always be evil, no matter what is chosen. When we analyse his concept of evil, we find a nicely excogitated concept, but one that simply means nothing. He says that if we do what the natural law commands, but do it with the slightest imperfection, then we have not observed the law, and the act is thus evil. The slightest inevitable egoism that influences my action vitiates it, and so even when I try to fulfill the law I break it and I sin. Calvin does not admit the Scholastic doctrine of lesser and greater sins in the sense that the lesser sin does not invalidate an act of fulfillment of the law. There are no venial sins for Calvin, if by that term we mean defective action which is still substantially sound. He will admit the term only in the sense that God can overlook any sin in those who confidently accept His promise to save men, by ignoring their sinfulness because of the merits of Jesus Christ. All this is logical if we admit Calvin's definition of the words, but it is so wearily beside the real points at issue.

We must remember that Calvin was a young man when he wrote the *Institutes*. It is true that he revised them as he grew older, but he was a tenacious man, and he did not take back what he had written in his youth. He had no love for the Church, and if we remember that his father lived and died under an excommunication imposed by that Church, we need not be surprised. Calvin knew how to read Latin and Greek as it was not read before the sixteenth century, and he "discovered" Paul in the living Greek and Augustine in the living Latin. He received a vital impact from these readings, and he never got the same impact from the duller Scholastic treatises that dealt with the writings of these same men.

Calvin never understood that he ended where the Scholastics had only begun. They carried on the investigation into the problems suggested by Paul and Augustine, who had not resolved them, and the Schoolmen made noteworthy advances. Calvin did not advance at all. He was not saying anything radically different from the tacit, implicit doctrine of the scholars who had preceded him, but he insisted that he was saying something different. They, whom he insulted on every occasion, were only too glad to understand him as stating what is really nonsense and what he did not really hold, so that it would be easy to hold him up to rejection and ridicule.

Even in the question of Predestination (which is not treated in the selections given in the Great Books Foundation text), Calvin was hardly as radical as he is often interpreted as being.

When his doctrine is finally boiled down (Book III, chaps. 21-24), Calvinistic Predestination is an application of the principle that nothing happens except what God for His own good motives wills, which is a truism. God wills some to be saved and He wills others not to be saved. To avoid an unpleasant shock, I have spontaneously substituted: "wills others not to be saved," for a formula Calvin had no hesitation in using: "wills others to be damned to Hell." There is something harsh about the latter way of expressing whatever truth there is in it, but Calvin thought he was being courageous, coherent and foursquare in saying it, because he was insensible to the manysidedness of truth and man's totality of reaction to half-truth expressions.

Calvin did not deny that the damned sinned freely. Calvin did not deny that there was no coaction, interior or exterior, in man's sinning. He did not deny that he did not know why God organized things thus, except that in some mysterious way He was manifesting his goodness and justice. If Calvin had tempered the harshness of his expression with the light of fuller truth, and if he had used the subtle but wise distinctions with which his predecessors had taught the same doctrine, he would not have been so bitterly criticised—but neither would he have been saying anything "new."

If Calvin was not original in his doctrine on man's present condition, an anthropological question solved from a theologian's point of view, he was certainly more original in dealing with the sociological question, the nature of human political society (Book IV, chap. 20). Calvin, like his Scholastic predecessors, distinguishes between two societies: the Christian community united by supernatural bonds, and the natural community of men linked by political ties. Now, it is important to insist at the outset that though Calvin distinguishes the two, yet he "separates" them far less than his Scholastic forerunners. The modern secularist will find more offense in Calvin that he will in St. Thomas Aquinas. For Thomas, the political society was bound together by, and acted for, the common good, which could be adequately defined by natural reason. For Calvin, the first purpose of the political union was to make possible the practice of Christian virtue, the defense of Christian doctrine in its purity, and the protection of Christian cult and ethics.

Now, when Calvin taught this, he was not thinking of some

kind of ideal goal toward which a State must tend. He made it
very clear when he was in power in Geneva that the political
society and its magistrates must here and now fulfill this primary
function of society. Between the years 1541 and 1546 he had
fifty-eight persons condemned to death and seventy-six sent to
exile. In 1547 Gruet was beheaded for "blasphemy," and in 1553
Servetus was burned at the stake for "heresy." The uprising of
the "Libertines," *i.e.,* those elements in Geneva politics who
were not docile to Calvin's ideas, was ruthlessly suppressed.

This sort of thing drives a modern reader to exasperation, and
he quite illogically cries: "A plague on both your houses! Get
religion out of politics." Strange as it may seem, though such
a cry would have been motive for exile in Calvin's Geneva,
Thomas Aquinas would have sympathised with it. He would
hardly have understood the phrase "keeping religion out of politics," with all the superstructure that the modern naturalist
imposes on it, but he would have insisted that the primary function of a political society was not the defense and protection of
a single religious group within the community. Thomas would
certainly have admitted such an obligation for certain societies,
not because of the end of the State, but because of the Catholic
faith of rulers and ruled in a totally Catholic collectivity. For
Thomas, State collaboration with one religious institution was
accidental, to be realized according to historical conditions. For
Calvin, State subservience to Calvinism was essential.

Yet Calvin had a definite influence in the production of modern democratic society. This is a simple fact. However, the Constitution of the United States is not a Calvinistic document, and
Calvin would have spurned some essential parts. The medieval
sociologists were nearer to the theory of the Constitution, and
the English and French philosophers of the Enlightenment were
nearer still.

How, then, did Calvin help to bring about the democratic
era? He was a congregationalist, and he rejected the notion of a
hierarchic constitution of classes as the framework of the visible
Church. In Calvinistic Christianity there were no clerics in the
medieval sense of the word, *i.e.,* a class by an inner abiding
power raised above other classes. For Calvin, the Church's external life was conducted by the community, not directly but by
freely elected, or at least popularly approved, officials who did

not differ in inner power from the other members of the congregation. The American Puritans were Calvinistic congregationalists, and they ran their civic affairs as they ran their church business, and the result was the New England Town Meeting. All men had a voice, and issues were decided by a show of hands. This is democratic procedure, and the American democracy as a social process was greatly indebted to New England Puritanism.

Indirectly, Calvin helped to bring on democracy. He was personally neither hostile to it nor in its favor. He repeats what Plato said, namely, that there are three forms of polity: monarchy, which can so easily turn into despotic tyranny; aristocracy, which by inner gravity slides readily into government for a single class; democracy, which under the pressure of contingencies dissolves into anarchy. Calvin, like St. Thomas, admits that any one of the three is a valid government; but unlike Thomas, who thought that the best government would combine the three forms into a fused system, Calvin states that he prefers an oligarchy. He calls it aristocracy, but he does not mean by that word what we mean today.

In this stand, Calvin shows how his time and temper played an important part in the formation of his philosophical views. He passionately disliked the notion of papacy, nor had he fared well at the hands of the French King, from whose power he had to flee. It was natural, then, that he should be antimonarchic. However, he had an unpleasant autocratic streak in his character. It manifests itself in his theology. For Calvin, arbitrary Election and Predestination, Justification by imputation, i.e., freedom from guilt not in fact but by decree, are all perfectly acceptable things, for no other reason than that the Supreme Lord, whose will is not only law but the measure of right and wrong, has willed them. Nothing is declared good or bad because of intrinsic structure, but because it is willed by God. Calvin's God does not will things because they are right and good; they are right and good because God wills them. These are the ideas of an autocrat.

As for democracy, Calvin could hardly feel for it. Democracy is based on optimism and the supposition that the people are wise. Calvin was a pessimist. He did not think that the people leaned to the good. On the contrary, because they were corrupt, they would lean to the bad. As for wisdom, so little is left in humanity that only a few exceptional men manifest anything like a respectable quantity of it. The people, as Calvin saw it, must be guided by religious persons. It is true that we are all free with the freedom of Christ, but as Calvin says against the Anabaptists, this holds only *in foro interno. In foro externo* we are not free at all. People must not rule, but rather they must be ruled, not harshly nor severely but with vigor and no laxity.

Oligarchy suited Calvin very well. It satisfied his distaste for monarchy but left ample scope for his autocracy. He could and did dominate the Geneva consistorium. This organ dominated Geneva. It was an excellent arrangement. No one could oppose Calvin, but yet he did not have to court popular favor as every monarch must do. Oligarchy ignored titles of nobility, and since Calvin had none, the Geneva bourgeois government gave him opportunities that a society tapering into nobility would have denied him disdainfully.

Calvin was not an original thinker, though he was a successful systematizer. He put together into one system the scattered elements of the sixteenth century. Nationalism was implicitly anti-papal, and Calvin rendered the implicit explicit. The New Learning was a philology, and Calvin, its product, made it substitute for the previous metaphysical theology by the simple expediency of making an ancient set of books the only source of belief. Antipapal revolution splintered the unity of the Church universal, and Calvin saved something of that unity by making the local congregation the social religious unit. He possessed no class superiority, and so he dissolved class distinction: in the Church, by abolishing hierarchical structure, and in civil society by saddling the people with an impersonal oligarchy. He did all this without being a revolutionary, for he retained all that the past offered and the present still conserved, provided that it be adjusted to his architectonic framework. The profounder elements of his theology he borrowed without compunction from the ancient tradition without change in substance, though he did change the rhetoric. This is the historical meaning of Calvin.

As a man, the brusque, rude Luther was far more loveable. His crudity, the fruit of spontaneity, was balanced by another fruit, flights of sublimity. The corruption of men, stressed far more emphatically by Luther than by Calvin, did not weigh so heavily on the German, who had many moments of genuine joy of life. Calvin was not spontaneous. He was controlled and aloof. His works show no spirit of doubt, and he considers his adversaries as fools or knaves. "Babblers," "sophists," "petulant," "murmurers," "virulent dogs," "blasphemers," "audacious," "infatuated," and a score of other epithets of like nature, are used coldly and generously for his opponents. He was a good hater, but he hated more with his intellect than with his heart. It never occurred to him to apply to himself the famous counsel of one of his later disciples, to bethink himself that he might be mistaken.

His morality was most strict, and he imposed it on others without any elasticity. Sobriety, industry, docility and bourgeois uniformity were cardinal virtues. His piety was ethical rather than ecstatic, and he had no patience with "revelations." He was loyal to his God, who was an arbitrary autocrat—but Calvin had won His favor, and consequently he had no fear. Whether or not his was a saving faith can be disputed, but at any rate, he lived up to it.

GUSTAVE WEIGEL

SELECTED BIBLIOGRAPHY

WARFIELD, Benjamin B., Calvin and Calvinism (ed. by E. D. Warfield). Oxford.
TORRANCE, Thomas F., Calvin's Doctrine of Man. London: Lutterworth Press.
MILES, Robert W., That Frenchman, John Calvin. New York: Revell.
BARRY, William, "Calvin," Catholic Encyclopedia, vol. iii, 195ff. Appleton.
SEIDER, Andreas, "Calvin," Lexikon für Theologie und Kirche. Bd. ii, 707ss., 1931.
    Freiburg i B.: Herder.
CALVIN, John, Institutes of the Christian Religion, Selections. Regnery.

Shakespeare: Macbeth

Macbeth is the spiritual autobiography of a man unable to assimilate the new Machiavellianism because of an undying orthodox conscience.

Many of the pivotal Renaissance problems are still with us, especially the concept of a monistic world, essentially depraved, to which "will" or the techniques of power are the key. Machiavelli accepted the thesis of late Augustinian theology about the depravity of man but divorced it from any theological context. Men will grow rogues on your hands unless by fear you compel them to be honest. Implicit in Machiavelli is the denial of Providence. We have before us a world of moral chaos in which the man of will, of *virtù*, can succeed where those who are crippled by ethics and conscience must fail. "Nature" is Edmund's "goddess" in *King Lear*—it is an "atheistic" nature, in which there is no supernatural referent. It is merely one cosmic matter ready to be mastered by the adventurer, the man of drive and virtuosity. The dualism of Christianity—implying the reality of a world of spirit as well as of matter, of eternity as well as of time, of universal justice as well as of will—is ignored by Machiavellians of the order of Edmund in *King Lear,* Iago in *Othello.*

Shakespeare, in dealing with history, presents contemporary. Elizabethan men preoccupied with the social ideas of the Renaissance. His history plays, as Lily B. Campbell has so painstakingly pointed out in *Shakespeare's "Histories"—Mirrors of Elizabethan Policy,* are actual commentaries by way of analogy and allegory on the immediate events that surrounded Shakespeare. In this respect, Macbeth stands at an historical crossroads. The new Machiavellian atheism and "naturalism" attract him; an almost mystic devotion to the power symbol obsesses him, but unlike Iago, he is unable to smother an orthodox conscience in the new cult of the will (as Iago puts it, "Virtue? a fig! 'Tis in our-selves that we are thus or thus.").

Not that Macbeth does not try. He applies Machiavellianism experimentally, only to rediscover empirically the validity of the supernatural world—*when it is too late*. *Macbeth* offers interesting parallels to Marlowe's *Tragical History of Dr. Faustus*. Both Faustus and Macbeth attempt to reduce the supernatural dimension to an instrument of personal power. All forces—God or devil—are available for the man of *virtù*. Both Faustus and Macbeth act with great shrewdness on the surface level, and with great stupidity on the universal and ultimate level. Both are judged by their creators, not by the canons of Machiavelli but by the traditional principles of Christianity. Dr. Faustus deliberately sought out and "juggled" with the fiends. His tragedy did not consist in the commission of that particular crime, but in his *explicit* despair. Macbeth juggles with the fiends at their express suborning. His tragedy does not consist in the chain of events that follows, but rather in the *implicit* despair that accompanies all his subsequent acts.

A great tragedy, whether in pagan Greece or in the declining Christianity of the Renaissance, depends upon the artist's ability to express the moral sense representing the universal experience of man. In spite of Socrates' optimism that man will do what is good if he *knows* what is good, great artists have emphatically shown how often men have known what is good and have chosen what is evil. Knowledge, in increasing the sense of responsibility, makes man more reluctant to commit evil, but by no means prevents him. From the Christian point of view, knowledge and will power are not in themselves sufficient for the good life. Grace is also necessary.

Macbeth, though he possesses a conscience, has an anthropocentric view of religion. The anthropocentric view reduces the possibilities of Grace. In this view, God and the supernatural are regarded as an instrument to man's ends. God becomes a convenient instrument, magical or propagandist, to aid the success of an individual, a class, a nation. The fact that man should be God's instrument to God's end is forgotten. The transcendence of God is ignored. Macbeth's religious sense in this respect has deep blind spots. The pagan philosopher who can at least think in terms of universals, such as justice or beauty, has more effective spiritual insight than a Christian like Macbeth who, disregarding his special graces, attempts to make the supernatural an instrument of personal power. This attempt is, of course, unintelligent on the deepest level. The transcendent cannot be so used. But then murder is unintelligent. The cult of power is unintelligent. Sin is unintelligent.

Machiavellianism is unintelligent. That is why, viewed purely as an intellectual pattern, the Machiavellian character is close to caricature and to laughter. That is why the medieval devil and even Milton's Satan hover at times between malevolence and comedy. Viewed in the cosmic light of universal principles, what *is* Satan's egoism worth? What does a crown matter? Who really cares if you are head of General Motors?

Because Macbeth is a Renaissance empiricist, who would turn religion into magic if he could, his spiritual sense is not deep. But Macbeth respects *power,* and his religious sense tends to concentrate specifically on *one* aspect of medieval tradition—the concept of the awful God of power, of retribution, of Judgment Day, of death and hell. This concept did not prove a sufficient safeguard, however, in the actual circumstances of Macbeth's temptation.

In considering specifically what that temptation was, space prevents an analysis of the relationship of the play to contemporary theological and juridical concepts of demonology. Walter Clyde Curry, in *Shakespeare's Philosophical Patterns,* has given an acute analysis of this background, a knowledge of which enriches our imaginative understanding of *Macbeth.* It is sufficient to note here that the play deals with demonology in a technical manner that undoubtedly pleased James I, Shakespeare's patron, an expert in the field. Contemporary demonology had absorbed large measures of superstition, and Shakespeare incorporates in his play some of the pessimism of the late Augustinian tradition. "Satan is prince of this world" constitutes a time-honored thesis in theology, but the late Augustinian tradition handed over practically the whole natural world to Satan. The demons, according to this view, controlled "nature's germens" (IV, i, 59)—the *rationes seminales*—the germinative causalities of the natural order, and their agents could foretell what grain would grow and what would not. Shakespeare, however, avoids the ultimate consequences of pessimism by maintaining the free will of man. Man can be the target of demonic temptation, but man's will is his own.

Shakespeare conceives of forces external to man awaiting the opportunity to use the potentialities of evil within man for his own destruction. The Weird Sisters, agents of Satan, echo what is within Macbeth's mind. They are fully aware of his dangerous love of power. As instruments of tragic "premonition," they appear and reappear to emphasize the demonic *motif* at climactic points in the play. Man knows the devil cannot be trusted, but the demonic voice can nevertheless be immediately seductive, especially when it correlates, as in this play, with the psychological weakness of the person tempted. As Banquo observes (I, iii, 122-126):

> ... But 'tis strange!
> And oftentimes, to win us to our harm,
> The instruments of darkness tell us truths,
> Win us with honest trifles, to betray's
> In deepest consequence.

Macbeth has desired and thought of the acquisition of the crown of Scotland, the power symbol, before he met these preternatural beings. Lady Macbeth indicates that her husband first suggested the crime (I, vii, 48-49). Without such interior inclination, Macbeth would not have been so affected by the Weird Sisters, but rather would have manifested the indifference of Banquo.

Unfortunately for Macbeth, temptation came to him from a more powerful source than that of the Weird Sisters. It came through the agency of his wife. The spirits of evil that are so close to the principals of this play are invoked in her determination to be inflexible of will. In pursuing the limited and materialistic objective of the crown, she comes dangerously near pleading for demonic *possession* (I, v, 41-44):

> ... Come, you spirits
> That tend on mortal thoughts, unsex me here
> And fill me from the crown to the toe, top-full
> Of direst cruelty!

Preternaturally reinforced to a *virtù* beyond her normal nature, she is coldly purposive with a taut intensity. Her unnatural coolness makes her completely practical, in so thorough a command

of the preparations for the killing of Duncan that she can afford
to advise and motivate her husband (I, v, 66-67):

> . . . look like the innocent flower
> But be the serpent under't.

But Macbeth's orthodox conscience does not die easily. Shakespeare has a profound understanding of the ways of temptation,
and the artistic skill to make the audience realize his knowledge.
The struggle in Macbeth is poignant and prolonged. When Macbeth is allowed a moment to think for himself, his conscience is
tormented acutely because of his powerful imagination, which
gives concrete and compelling symbols to his fears (I, vii, 21-25):

> And pity, like a naked new-born babe,
> Striding the blast, or heaven's cherubim, hors'd
> Upon the sightless couriers of the air,
> Shall blow the horrid deed in every eye,
> That tears shall drown the wind.

His wife's unnatural will wins Macbeth's admiration, easily impressed as he is by power, and weighs the balance in favor of
the murder. Macbeth catches the infection of her hysterical will,
concluding in a tense and ominous calm (I, vii, 79-80):

> . . . I am settled, and bend up
> Each corporal agent to this terrible deed.

Macbeth lives through an experience before it arrives; his
senses are those of a poet, and he must pay the double penalty
of anticipation and realization. There is a complex and perverted courage in a man of Macbeth's nervous intensity actually
committing a murder. For him, even the castle stones are alive
with pulsating consciousness (II, i, 57-59):

> . . . Thou sure and firm-set earth,
> Hear not my steps, which way they walk, for fear
> Thy stones prate of my whereabout . . .

Macbeth realizes so well what he is doing. He experiences the
full horror of conscious sin, unclouded by ignorance.

It is the moral enormity of the murder that is the theme of
the great scenes of *Macbeth*. It is an order of reality which Machiavellianism cannot penetrate. Shakespeare, with macabre dramatic power, has underlined the ironic nature of evil, its capacity

to make use of noble qualities to cut man off from the source, not only of these original qualities, but of life itself. Macbeth's sensitivity, imagination, courage are great qualities. Entering into an ironic and perverted relationship with evil, self-consumed to ashes, these qualities cast a dying light through the thickening menace of "the great doom's image" (II, iii, 83).

Once committed, the murder awakens a brief but penetrating insight into the transcendent in Macbeth's conscience. Macbeth overhears the guards of the King talking in their sleep. Bravado-like, to test his nerve, Macbeth attempts to say "Amen" (II, ii, 27-30):

> One cried "God bless us!" and "Amen" the other,
> As they had seen me with these hangman's hands.
> List'ning their fear, I could not say "Amen!"
> When they did say "God bless us!"

For a moment he sees the chaos of sin. The blood on his hands plucks out his eyes. Extremely powerful is that word, heavy with associated horror, that Shakespeare creates, *incarnadine* (II, ii, 61-63):

> . . . No, this my hand will rather
> The multitudinous seas incarnadine
> Making the green one red.

In his realization of guilt, Macbeth is on a transcendently different level from that of Lady Macbeth. She says, "a little water clears us of this deed," but Macbeth knows that "all great Neptune's ocean" will not wash the blood clean from his hand. Dramatically appropriate is the knocking at the gate in this atmosphere of naked nerves—the big, jarring knocking. Yet it is the blood in the darkness that is more horrible, that is louder than any knock, the blood that plucked out Macbeth's spiritual eyes.

Not a good adjustment for a Machiavellian! Turning to *The Prince* (Chapter VIII: "Of Those Who Have Attained the Position of Prince by Villainy"), we read:

I believe this [maintenance of the prince's power] arises from the cruelties being exploited well or badly. Well committed may be called those (if it is possible to use the word well of evil) which are perpetrated once for the need of securing one's self, and which afterwards are not persisted in, but are exchanged for measures as useful to the subjects as possible. Cruelties ill committed are those which, although at first few, increase rather than diminish with time.

Macbeth, in thinking of the cosmic meaning of evil in terms of Christian tradition, is seriously failing in the technical aspects of Machiavellianism. He does not kill *all* his possible enemies at one blow but, paralyzed by a Christian conscience, proceeds piecemeal, allowing opposition to cement against him, the political consequences of which are lengthily considered in terms of the new political science (including Malcolm's conspiratorial approach to Macduff) in Act IV.

There is no greater scene in Shakespeare than Act II, Scene ii for tension and intensity of symbolism. Macbeth has not only struck a mortal blow at a king; he has killed his own membership in the "great chain of being" of Christian tradition. He has negated the Communion of Saints, the cosmic harmony so beloved of Renaissance thinkers.

As a tragic character, Macbeth is a failure in two worlds, the Machiavellian and the Christian. He would have been content to settle for the public acclaim that habitually accompanies "power" and "*virtù*." But he has been in too intimate a contact with orthodox tradition to allow this settlement. He can distinguish "mouth-honour" from love. Macbeth's mind is not simple enough, unilateral enough for thoroughgoing Machiavellianism, though subtle enough for its practices, as distinct from its intellectual foundations. Macbeth can at times be as capable and as efficient an executive as Claudius in *Hamlet* (also a regicide) but he has a spiritual insight that Claudius never approached. Claudius was simply Machiavellian. Macbeth, acting as a Machiavellian, could not extinguish his sense of Christian justice.

Macbeth's retribution is internal rather than external. He is the witness to the degeneration of his own soul. Macbeth has "murdered sleep," all that is implied in the symbolism of that word . . . to discover that life is a "tale told by an idiot." Macbeth empirically proves to himself that the life to come cannot be "jump'd." Shakespeare knows that the supernatural is organically linked to the natural; the Machiavellian divorce is as impossible as the Cartesian divorce.

It might be urged, could not Macbeth repent? Shakespeare

understood the meaning of contrition and mercy, as in the famous Portia speech and in that of Claudius (*Hamlet*, III, iii). in this sense, *Macbeth* is a tragedy of implicit despair. Repentance means a spiritual revolution; it means a turning back upon a way of life. It is not an easy or mechanical act. Claudius, whatever his villainy, was well instructed in orthodoxy and knew that he could not both repent and retain the effects of sin. For Macbeth, likewise, repentance is practically impossible (though possible in theory) because, in fullness of knowledge, he has deliberately chosen the level on which he is to live. The point is reached in his spiritual life where there is no motivation except fear (as in *Dr. Faustus*) for the act of repentance. But fear, if degeneration has gone far enough, is more than neutralized by boredom and despair. Macbeth has chosen to live on a specific level—in his case, the Machiavellian. Such a choice implies a rejection of all values, all truths, that oppose this level. Just as one might decide that money or prestige or pleasure is the only thing that counts in society, Macbeth has chosen "sovereign sway." Macbeth deliberately acquiesces in his own self-blindness (III, iv, 136-137):

> ... For my own good
> All causes shall give way.

His concept of "good" is by this time quite ironic, as ironic as the lines in which Faustus tells Mephistopheles to "learn of Faustus manly fortitude." Shakespeare, like Milton, has the artistic skill to show the correlation between the performance of evil and increasing intellectual blindness.

Does Macbeth win our pity as the purposes of Aristotelian tragedy dictate he should? There is no doubt in Macbeth's case about the tragic fault, about his criminality. But has he not himself paid a terrible penalty in disillusionment, and are we not under obligation to him for what he has told us about evil? He attempted to handle the preternatural world in terms of personal power. He made a paradoxical effort, similar to that of Dr. Faustus, to subordinate the supernatural to material aims, only to find himself a king of nothing. His death—he dies spiritually before he dies physically—is a poignant moral lesson, underlining in its deepest aspects the meaning of evil.

WILLIAM J. GRACE

SELECTED BIBLIOGRAPHY

BRADLEY, A. C., *Shakesperean Tragedy*. Macmillan.
CAMPBELL, Lily B., *Shakespeare's Tragic Heroes: Slaves of Passion*. Cambridge.
CAMPBELL, Lily B., *Shakespeare's "Histories"—Mirrors of Elizabethan Policy*. Huntington Library.
CURRY, Walter Clyde, *Shakespeare's Philosophical Patterns*. Louisiana State University Press.
DE QUINCEY, Thomas, *On the Knocking at the Gate in Macbeth*.
KNIGHT, G. W., *Wheel of Fire: Essays in Interpretation of Shakespeare's Sombre Tragedies*. Oxford.
QUILLER-COUCH, Sir A., *Shakespeare's Workmanship*. Cambridge.
SPENCER, Theodore, *Shakespeare and the Nature of Man*. Macmillan.
SPURGEON, C. F. E., *Shakespeare's Imagery*. Macmillan.
SHAKESPEARE, William, *Tragedies*. Random House (Modern Library).
SHAKESPEARE, William, *Macbeth*. Regnery.

Milton: Paradise Lost

JOHN MILTON's was one of the most complex personalities of that exceedingly complicated period which we call the Renaissance. Conscious from early boyhood of exceptional intellectual gifts, he set about developing these as fully as possible, with the serious purpose of sharing them with others through teaching and writing. His attempt at full development was broad, embracing a study of music and politics, poetry and theology, languages and philosophy. His learning is astounding. When one has scanned the handbooks and compendia that were available during his time, one still feels that he was not content with these, but used them rather as bibliographical aids, going from them to the entire works that promised to be most valuable to him. In amassing his intellectual fortune, Milton was aided by a phenomenal memory rendered keener by necessity as his sight failed.

Probably two of his most obvious limitations were due in part to his voracious study. The fact that he was an eclectic rather than a profoundly original thinker may be a result of study so extensive that he was unable to give to his acquisitions the long and deep thought to which he might have subjected a smaller store. It is possible, on the other hand, that he was sincerely satisfied with the patterns he wove from chosen borrowings. To the studious seclusion of his boyhood may also be due his tendency to be academic in his treatment even of the most intimate human experiences: it is almost as though he were standing by with a stop-watch to count a lover's pulse. The rare passages in which he breaks through this shell of objectivity make one regretful for the human potentialities too often lost to his work.

In considering these limitations, however, the reader should bear in mind that Milton did not intend to propose a new theological system: novelty for its own sake did not appeal to him. Neither did he set out to tell in *Paradise Lost* merely a deeply

emotional story. His avowed purpose—and we have neither reason nor right to say that the avowal was not sincere—was "to
justify the ways of God to man," to instruct man first of all in
the motives not only of God's wrath but also of His mercy, and
over and above this, or rather, concomitantly with it and as a
necessary ancillary exposition, to instruct man in his own nature
and his obligations toward God, neighbor and self.

This didactic aim was in keeping with literary tradition. However gripping the epic in itself, it was regarded by Renaissance
readers as an illustration of the virtues of a great and noble
character under almost superhuman difficulties, and as an inspiration to greater nobility in the life of the reader.

It was because of the instructive and ennobling power of poetry that Milton in *Areopagitica* dared be known to think
Spenser "a better teacher than Aquinas," and not because he
despised the great philosopher. For Spenser had undertaken to
illustrate by action the twelve moral virtues of Aristotle and to
present, as well, whatever else was most necessary to the making
of a Christian gentleman. It may be that Milton, in completing
the systematic theology for which he had commenced making
notes during his young manhood, and writing an epic which
would incorporate its findings in beautiful and dynamic form,
conceived himself to be combining the functions of a Protestant
Aquinas and a more exalted Spenser. At any rate, *Paradise Lost*
rarely deviates theologically from the *Treatise on Christian
Doctrine,* as it is now called; and it illustrates the nature of man,
his virtues and responsibilities, as described in the prose work.
In selecting such material for his most ambitious works, Milton
was taking a direct, though laborious, way to fulfil what he had
set forth in his letter to Samuel Hartlib as the highest aim of
education: to "repair the ruins of our first parents by regaining
to know God aright, and out of the knowledge to love him, to
imitate him, to be like him."

It is in the portion of his work that deals directly with the
Trinity that Milton turns most sharply from traditional Christianity. In spite of persistent admonitions that God did not intend man to know all things, that some truths were to be left
uninvestigated, he seems to have been unable to accept so great
a mystery as the Trinity on the testimony of the New Testament, embracing instead the heretical opinion that the Son of

God was a creature of the Father, albeit the first and infinitely highest. It should be noted that he did regard the Son as partaking in some way of the divinity of the Father, though rather by gift than in essence—and not merely as an extraordinarily holy but exclusively human being, as is sometimes intimated. His ascription of the work of creation to the Son was neither heretical nor new.

A second deviation from the traditional pattern of Christian theology is his acceptance of the thoroughly Protestant doctrine of the imputation of the merits of Christ to fallen man instead of His vicarious atonement for man's sins.

But on a third point of theology, and the one which most vitally concerns the trend of his epic, Milton is as orthodox as St. Thomas himself: man is not arbitrarily predestined to salvation or damnation, he declares; every man receives sufficient grace—sufficient in the technical sense as understood by Catholic theologians, sufficient divine support to enable him to save his soul—and if he cooperates in spirit and in deed with this grace, he will be saved. Beyond this sufficiency, God may give yet more abundant grace to some than to others. Since all grace is a gratuitous gift, He is in no wise constrained by justice to give to all alike.

When we come to the question of the exact nature of this grace, again we find Milton somewhat vague. Whether he intended to intimate that it merely supports the soul in the manner of added strength, or that it actually changes and elevates it, as Catholic theologians taught, cannot be fully determined either from *Paradise Lost* or from the *Treatise on Christian Doctrine*. It is quite possible that Milton had not succeeded in answering the question to his own satisfaction, and that he passed over it as being of little practical importance.

What mattered most in this connection was the justification of the mercy of God in giving grace to fallen man and the insistence, with Catholic theologians and the heretic Arminius, upon the freedom of man's will to correspond with grace or to reject it. With regard to the first point, Milton reiterated the argument of the Fathers of the Church that man, having fallen not through his own malice but at the instigation of a wily enemy of superior strength, was worthy of a degree of lenience. At the same time, he had sinned against the infinite goodness of God, rendering himself at once accountable for an infinite wrong and incapable of any meritorious action by which to make satisfaction for his sin. This dilemma was to be solved by the Son of God, Who would take upon Himself a humanity untouched by the sin of Adam and render to God in Adam's name the perfect service that is His due. His merits would be imputed to Adam, making possible the restoration of anyone who availed himself of them.

Freedom, Milton insisted, was an essential quality of man—one of the dominant aspects of the image of God to which he was created—and could not have been lost without an essential change of nature. According to man's free rejection of grace or correspondence with it, he would be lost or saved.

The theological outlines of the epic are presented in the first three books, to be enlarged upon as the story unfolds. In narrating the fall of man, Milton treats the questions ordinarily considered by Biblical commentators. Perhaps because he at first considered presenting his great theme in the form of a drama, he concerns himself at the beginning with the matters of scene, motivation and character. True to conventional dramatic procedure, he does not introduce his major character, man, in the first act, but instead sets about establishing the fatherhood of God in all His justice and mercy, the heaven for which man is destined and whose inhabitants will do all possible in his interests, and the villain, Satan, with the hell to which he wishes to reduce the latest creature of God.

Milton's presentation of God cannot be said to be altogether successful: it is at once anthropomorphic and nebulous. Moreover, since God acts only by His will, He has fewer dramatic possibilities in the epic than has the devil, who is intensely and physically active. This may account in part for some of the misapprehensions of many readers concerning Milton's Satan. In judging Milton's characterization of the two antagonists, God and Satan, one should not ignore the analogy of the generally more dramatic character of evil than of good in the world itself. Furthermore, Satan was to be pitted against the Son of God, and so for dramatic purposes must be a creature of considerable magnitude. But the underlying fact which makes the character of Milton's Satan logical and, for the most part, consistent with all that we know of him from the Scriptures, is the quality of the angelic nature itself.

It is quite possible that Milton had read the famous tract of St. Thomas on the angels, although he could have derived the material for the character of Satan from any of the demonologies common in his day. Certainly the angel Raphael's description of the knowledge of angels reads like a versification of St. Thomas's explanation of it. But whatever the source of his knowledge, Milton adheres to the traditional concept of devils as fallen angels who, however debased by sin, nevertheless possess an essentially higher nature than man. Although they are morally lower than he, by reason of their lack of grace, they retain the essentials of their angelic nature—their incorporeality and their superior and intuitive knowledge, in particular—which give them certain advantages over man.

Milton's age was still close enough to the vivid awareness of the other world, the logic and the theology of England's Catholic ages, to understand all this. In another century, Humanism and a relaxed Protestantism would have carried the minds of most educated Englishmen to the point where Satan would be regarded as a magnificent figure exalted to heroic proportions by a poet who unconsciously admired him or found in him vicarious expression for his own arrogance. A century later, the Satan of the epic was to be admired because he had the courage to rebel. But anyone who reads attentively the whole of *Paradise Lost* will be aware that Milton finds it a degrading and despicable thing to rebel against the all-holy and all-loving God, and that as Satan continues in evil he loses even the horrible inverted dignity which he possesses at the opening of the epic.

In presenting Adam and Eve, Milton suffers something of the difficulty that confronted him in his delineation of God. It is impossible for man, as he has been since Adam, to imagine man as he was created by God, endowed with brilliance without arrogance, dignity without pride, enjoyment of all the natural goods of life without inordinate desire. Yet Milton strives to give a credible picture of our first parents, and if until the Fall it seems little more than a picture, it is nevertheless a picture of considerable beauty and poignancy.

At this point again, some acquaintance with the *Treatise on Christian Doctrine* is of value to the reader of *Paradise Lost*. In his prose work, Milton devoted considerable space to the virtues. Perhaps because it is basically Aristotelian, it is not unlike St.

Thomas's exposition of the virtues in his *Summa Theologica*. Turning from the abstract discussion, in prose, of these right habits of man, one finds them illustrated in the speech and actions of the first human beings as they appear in *Paradise Lost* —worship of God, responsibility for subordinates, pursuit of the natural knowledge of things pertaining to man's use and delight, mutual love and care of husband and wife, even the virtues of hospitality (in their entertainment of Raphael) and of urbanity in the gentle ceremoniousness of their address. Adam seems particularly gifted with prudence, which fails him in the end because of his too-great gregariousness.

Like more profound theologians, Milton is unable to explain fully how creatures so perfect could have fallen; but he manages to make the Fall credible. We have been made aware of the might and malice of the enemy, and we have surmised, from Adam's slightly adolescent part in the conversation with Raphael, that during the brief period before the Fall he has enjoyed the delights of the garden without probing deeply the perfections of the spiritual garden of his own soul. When the fallen Eve, led astray by her curiosity and vanity, entices Adam to eat of the forbidden fruit, he falls with appalling promptness. Since Adam is the head and progenitor of the human race, to whom all excellence has been given in trust for his posterity, his fall entails the fall from felicity of all mankind. The results of his action as presented by Milton are so perfectly in keeping with the traditional analysis that they need be no more than mentioned here—concupiscence, shame, deceit, recriminations, physical suffering, death and, implicitly at least, every evil that will befall man to the end of time.

Paradoxically, it is only when Adam has become least worthy of admiration and love that he becomes an emotionally sympathetic character. As the unfallen future father of the race, he is austere, noble and something of a prig; but with his capitulation to temptation—because he cannot bear to be alone—he becomes an individual human being confronted first with loneliness and then with an overwhelming sense of guilt and all the frustration and fear that memory of sin entails. Examining his case, he is forced to admit the justice of God's wrath and is driven almost to despair. His relentlessly clear mind repudiates every expedient—including suicide and refusal to bring children into the world—that he or Eve can propose for avoiding the penalty for their sin, either in themselves or in their posterity, and he admonishes his wife not to be too distressed over the "loss of life and pleasure overlov'd."

Adam's grief over his private misfortune is diverted into a deeper and nobler channel by the vision of the future shown him by Michael, in which he sees not only the evil brought by his sin upon the world, but the holiness of the few of his descendants who will strive to be faithful to their understanding of the will of God. Reduced at last to humility and peace, he is reminded by the archangel that to his new-found knowledge he must add deeds and the virtues of faith, patience, temperance and love, through which he will be able to substitute, for the external Paradise which he is about to leave, "a Paradise within thee happier far." With this solemn reassurance in his mind and comforted by the promise of ultimate victory over the serpent, he and Eve pass, gravely but confidently, into the outer world.

There is nothing unique in Milton's having chosen the Creation and Fall of man as the subject for his epic, but he stands alone among modern writers in having given it perennially impressive form. This is not to say that *Paradise Lost* is uniformly exalted poetry. It contains long stretches of prosaic exposition, and there are other passages in which an obviously poetic intention achieves an almost humorous effect, as in the description of the architecture of heaven and the anachronistic account of the war of the angels. If there is intentional humor in the poem, it appears in an occasional sly smile at the vanity of Adam and in what must have been a purposely awkward two lines about "th' unwieldly elephant" who

> To make them mirth, us'd all his might, and wreath'd
> His lithe proboscis . . .

But if we are to judge *Paradise Lost* as it should be judged— as a formal narrative in twelve books written in the most solemn of English meters, unrhymed iambic pentameter, to teach through contemplation of a noble story nobly told—we shall see it as a highly dramatic whole illumined by carefully integrated passages of great beauty, such as those depicting the inverted magnificence of Satan, the innocence and wonder with which

Adam and Eve recount their first memories of earth, Eve among her roses shortly before her tragic encounter with the serpent, the withered garland in the hand of Adam, the moral ugliness and mutual recriminations following the Fall and, finally, the sorrowful pair wandering slowly down the outer slope of the Garden of Eden.

SISTER MARY IRMA, B. V. M.

SELECTED BIBLIOGRAPHY

MILTON, John, *The Complete Poetry and Selected Prose of*. Random House (Modern Library).

MILTON, John, *Paradise Lost*. Merritt Y. Hughes, ed. Odyssey Press.

HANFORD, James H., *A Milton Handbook*. 4th edition. Crofts.

KELLEY, Maurice, *This Great Argument*. Princeton.

LEWIS, Clive S., *A Preface to Paradise Lost*. Oxford.

TILLYARD, E. M. W., *Milton*. Macmillan.

WHITING, George, *Milton's Literary Milieu*. University of North Carolina Press.

MILTON, John, *Paradise Lost*. Regnery.

Locke: Essay Concerning Human Understanding

IN READING and discussing *Of Civil Government (The Great Books,* Vol. I), it was probably observed that John Locke has a rather up-to-date, even contemporary air about him. The same thing is true in the case of the *Essay.* This is not, of course, because John Locke is contemporary, but because our contemporary philosophic language has been so much influenced by his *Essay Concerning Human Understanding.*

This contemporary air is especially marked in Book Three. Much attention is given to overcoming semantic difficulties, as we should now say, by striking at their root causes. He is pleading, and genially, for a common understanding of the nature of language itself. He gives us a system for understanding it by distinguishing words from ideas, general from particular, what is really essence from essence only in name. By all this he hopes to avoid or diminish confusion in communication. Further, he is insistent about the claims of the concrete against the abstract, with an insistence deeply rooted in his friendly and tolerant character. He thus pleads for a great deal of toleration about the language of religion and morality. All this contrives to give the new or repeating reader of Locke a rather exhilarating sense of familiarity. This is quite understandable because, although his philosophic importance is by no means as great today as it was one or two centuries ago, it is precisely as a philosopher of knowledge that "the gentle physician" makes his chief and abiding claim to fame.

As with every other philosopher, however (and, indeed, every great book), Locke's claim to be heard should not be estimated by contemporary influence, but by the simple truth and importance of what he has to say. This is what makes reading a philosopher such an absorbing job. Precisely as a philosopher he offers us truth—and important truth. And if he expressly claims that what he has to say is the truth, who are you, or who am I, to say it is not so? We can read a philosopher only philosophically. To do this, one must keep an eye on his questions, his evidences, his method. One should find out from him 1) what problems or questions he would like to solve; 2) what he accepts as true, as clear, as indispensable in solving them, and 3)—this is most important—how does he propose to go about it?

"After all those praters had written the romance of the soul," Voltaire said, contrasting John Locke with men far greater than Locke and himself, "a wise man came along and wrote its history."

That is Voltaire's description of Locke's answer to the last of those three questions. You will find Locke himself describing his procedure as an "historical, plain method."

"Historical method," as Locke uses it, is not exactly "historical" as you, or Thucydides, or Mr. Toynbee, might mean it. It is historical, rather, as Aristotle, for instance, uses the word historical in "the history of animals." Locke's theory of knowledge is very largely a kind of descriptive anatomy of consciousness. He is justly proud of its simplicity, its plainness. And because the anatomy of consciousness, or the structure of knowledge, is at its plainest and its plainly describable best at the level of sense knowledge, John Locke did a very brilliant job of dissecting and describing sense knowledge.

Locke liked his method, of course. He liked it so much, and liked it at its best so much, that it is pretty hard to see whether any knowledge but sense knowledge remains when Locke gets through with his historical, plain method.

With regard to the first of our three points-to-watch, one will not find John Locke being so confident about his originality. He is readily contented that the questions and problems of philosophy are well established: the soul, the external world, and God.

Such a set-up of questions and problems was, in fact, far from original with Locke. Malebranche, Leibnitz, Spinoza—very great men all—had dealt with those problems. How to deal with them, they had learned from René Descartes. But they used Descartes's method; each used it in his own variation; none of them used the historical, plain method of John Locke. On the other hand, neither did they take the soul, or God, or the external world for granted. Each of those four men gave his own rigorous account of the soul, of God, of the external world. And each was very precise about the evidence which must be accepted in giving his account of the soul, God, and the world.

This brings us to the second of our points-to-watch, our three questions to bring to the reading of Locke (or any philosopher). Was he precise about accepting and rigorous in examining his evidences?

There is good reason to suppose that Locke was not. Let us put it this way. Descartes proved: a) the soul is a thinking substance; b) the infinite, omniscient God exists; c) extended substance, called body, exists and is knowable. Whether or not all those conclusions are questionable (and they have all been thoroughly questioned) and whether or not they are true (and as Descartes understood the first, many of us consider it false), nevertheless, they *are* conclusions. They are not evidences. Descartes never thought they were. They are not starting points, but terms. But Descartes did not reach them by Locke's historical, plain method.

Neither did John Locke. He did not reach those conclusions, he started from them. Now, it is a curious but rigid rule in the history of philosophy that conclusions not only are no better than the method by which they are reached, but also cannot abide without that method. Physician John Locke would approve our figure if we put it this way: the conclusions are the philosophy's complexion, its "clinical appearance"; but the method is its blood stream. And the organism without its own healthy blood will not long have a healthy appearance. This is the very reason why those good healthy Cartesian conclusions, separated by Locke from the Cartesian method, fade, faint and waste away before your very eyes.

Take the thinking substance, soul. The historical, plain method, specializing in sense knowledge, leaves us with no very good "idea" of soul. Therefore, thinking or not, Cartesian or not, the soul arrived at by this method will not stand up under criticism for long.

Take God, the cause and creator of the universe for Christians —and Locke was a good Christian. But no man can acquire much knowledge of God in accordance with an anatomy of knowledge that is very plain about sense knowledge and rather vague about every other kind. Hence the uneasy feeling that arises about Locke's proof of God's existence. Is it really worth much? —the inquiring reader may ask. Like everyone else, including John Locke, one has to answer that it is not.

And that extended and knowable substance, body? When, following Locke's brilliant analysis of sensory knowledge, one has peeled off all the knowability that substance has by Locke's method, one will very seriously question whether there is any substance there to be known. No doubt, Locke meant his subtle and brilliant analysis of sensory knowledge to work like the peeling of an apple or an orange. Instead, it works like a very, very thorough peeling of an onion.

To grasp the method of a philosopher is truly to enter into his pursuit of wisdom. One does not always find him insisting upon his characteristic method, in fact not every philosopher is as explicit about his procedure as John Locke. And his explicit treatment is not found in the treatment of words in Book Three. The method is at that point both established and clarified. In Book Three the reader finds rather results of the method than clarification.

Thus one finds Locke taking the "Natural Philosophers" to task for failure in precision about their ideas. He gives a genial scolding to those who speak of matter and body without adding to the clarity and distinctness of our ideas or exhibiting much clarity and distinctness of their own. Contemporary readers may find this rather puzzling, the more so if they recall that Locke was on friendly terms with the scientific men of his day. But anyone can look within himself and discover that the more vivid is his purely sensory knowledge the more it defies universal formulization. Locke is here only faithful to his method.

Throughout the passage, Locke takes any knowledge or pretended knowledge of substance or essence as an established and notorious source of confusion and error. Physician and lover of the concrete that he was, he respects the working of nature and that "real Constitution" whereby everything is what it is and on which its "sensible Qualities depend." Why then object to substance or essence?

The method of knowledge cannot explain them. Why then

so readily admit substance and essence in other guises as realities with which language, art, science and philosophy may deal? Locke could admit matter, body, substance, essence because along with his own method he embraced—as already said—the conclusions of Descartes. The incompatibility of those conclusions with his method gives the curious results of Book Three: on the one hand a confident, common-sense vigor in treating the problems of language; on the other, sharply dogmatic limits on language's power to communicate. For if body is but my idea of body, how can men communicate about body? And if any idea of substance is of little worth, are not men in difficulty about agreement as to what is substantial?

It may seem that we are leaving John Locke with some very pale and unhealthy conclusions, indeed. Perhaps we are. We need not press the point. We do leave him with his historical, plain method. A surprise awaits readers of the Great Books in the fourth year when they see what David Hume, with a method which he derived from John Locke, does to those Lockian evidences which are really Cartesian conclusions.

We have been speaking here, actually, only of Locke's method, and have been indicating how the reader of the *Essay* can appraise it. He will find it worthless for establishing happiness and virtue as principles of the good life (as Aristotle does in his *Ethics*) or in fathoming the grounds of law as an intelligible principle of guidance (as St. Thomas does). Locke's method is not the key to the beauty of justice as Plato saw it, nor to the beauty of religion as Pascal defined it.

John Locke's plain method is the key to John Locke, of course. And from him one can learn that it is far more important for wisdom to be plainly open, plainly generous and plainly humble than just plain! One can learn above all that wisdom must be free to embrace, to use knowledge to grow in and by every knowledge and every form of knowledge; that bondage to any limited method and body of conclusions—even bondage to the senses most brilliantly and thoroughly anatomized—destroys wisdom's liberty and beauty; that the very beauty and liberty of human wisdom are one with her hunger for the vast infinite range of being, the good, and the true.

CHARLES J. O'NEIL

SELECTED BIBLIOGRAPHY

LOCKE, John, *Essay Concerning Human Understanding*, edited by A. C. Fraser, 2 vols. Oxford.

BURTT, Edwin A., editor, *The English Philosophers from Bacon to Mill*. Random House (Modern Library).

GILSON, Étienne, *The Unity of Philosophical Experience*. Scribner.

GILSON, Étienne, *Being and Some Philosophers*. Toronto, Ontario: Pontifical Institute of Mediaeval Studies.

LOCKE, John, *Essay Concerning Human Understanding*. Regnery.

Voltaire: Candide

AN UNCONFIRMED REPORT has it that Voltaire locked himself up in his room and wrote Candide in *three* days. Perhaps he did, for the work has all the earmarks of a brilliant and rapid improvisation: a quick and sprightly agility, a rapidly allusive and nervous style and an apparently inexhaustible wealth of color, movement and imagination. We can well believe that when the original idea had matured sufficiently in his head, Voltaire set pen to paper and suddenly, as the words came to him, knew that he was in perfect form, that his work was coming to life, and that his verve and inspiration were working at their best and easiest. At such moments of good fortune, it is of course fatal to interrupt the happy flow of felicitous words, and it is then not at all improbable that Voltaire did indeed lock himself in his room in order to give the creative process free rein.

In any case, whether the actual composition of the work took three days or three months, it had indeed been very long in the preparation. The elements of the tale are not too difficult to find for those conversant with Voltaire's life and his reading up to this point. His sojourn at the Prussian Court of Frederick the Great, his sharp and shrewd observations there, and finally his disappointed bitterness as he left it, furnish the "Westphalian" background of the tale. All the various adventures, misfortunes, tribulations and sufferings of its characters, their travels to Lisbon, Buenos Aires, Paraguay, "El Dorado," Venice and Constantinople, the *motifs* of war, pillaging, rapine, kidnaping into slavery, disguises, reappearance of "dead" brothers, friends, lovers, etc., as well as many of the descriptions and reflections inspired by these voyagings, all were literary commonplaces of the time.

But aside from all the trappings of exoticism and melodrama, and the generous dash of spicy, off-color salaciousness, *Candide,* like all of Voltaire's tales, is essentially concerned with ideas. And these ideas, too, had long been in his mind and in those of his contemporaries, for the eighteenth centry was the "philosophical" century *par excellence*—not only in France, but in England, Germany and even the young English colonies of North America.

After the religious anarchy of the seventeenth century which followed the religious revolt against the authority of the Church in the sixteenth, men began to question ideas more basic than details of religious doctrine and practice. They began to doubt in ever-increasing numbers whether there was really any such thing as a revealed religion; some went so far as to doubt, or even to deny, that there was a God. And those who did maintain a belief in Him, but were deprived of the light of revelation, began to reexamine the fundamental questions of His nature, His goodness and its relation to the existence of evil in the world, His omnipotence and its relation to both the existence of evil and the freedom of the human will. These great philosophical questions, considered purely in the light of human reason, have probably never been a matter of such general preoccupation in intellectual circles as they were in the eighteenth century, at least not since the time of the early Greek philosophers.

With his voracious reading, his incessant social and literary activity, and his ultrasensitive reactions to all currents of thought and feeling about him, Voltaire could not but play his part and say his often-decisive word in these debates. And *Candide* is, accordingly, full of memories and reflections of, and allusions to, these contemporary themes, arguments, quarrels and personal resentments and bickering, as the masterful edition by Professor André Morize has so amply shown.

It was impossible, however, for Voltaire to remain very long on the level of abstract philosophical thought; ideas, for him, were always incarnated in the persons of their proponents and in the individual entities or facts which served to illustrate or to combat them. And Voltaire never got very far from the individual concrete fact. "Man," he was convinced, "is not equipped to understand the essential nature of things; he can only calculate, measure, weigh and experiment." In other words, our only form of real knowledge is that which is concerned with material things, which lend themselves to the empirical and experimental approach indicated by the four verbs in this quotation from one of his letters. Any attempt to understand, much less to affirm, general truths in regard to basic, underlying metaphysical questions is foredoomed to failure.

Metaphysics, he affirmed elsewhere, is concerned with only two kinds of things: first, things which all men of common sense already know, and second, things which we will never know. For Voltaire is fundamentally and consciously opposed in principle to any and all metaphysics, and not merely to any particular one. In writing his *Candide*, however, since he was not a man to deal with general ideas in abstract terms, he deals with them in terms of the particular metaphysical questions and problems which were most familiar to him and to the men of his day.

The one problem which was most basic in both the moral and the metaphysical order was surely the perennial problem of evil. In the first half of the eighteenth century it had been revived under the new and special aspect of the debate on the question of the philosophical "optimism" of Leibnitz and his disciples. Its most important and influential proponent in the literary sphere was undoubtedly Alexander Pope, in his *Essay on Man* in particular. Leibnitz maintained that an omnipotent, wise and good God could not, at the moment of Creation, have chosen any but the best of all possible worlds, and that therefore all the evils of which we are aware are indisputably necessary parts of the best of all possible worlds, and in some way which may or may not be clear to us, fit into and contribute to the goodness of the whole. And Pope expressed a similar thought in his more pithy, if more imprecise, poetical language: "Whatever is, is right." Voltaire's early sojourn in England had acquainted him intimately with the various currents in English literary and philosophical thinking, and we know that he was well acquainted with Pope's works.

When Voltaire does battle against metaphysics, then, he chooses the particular metaphysics at hand, the one which is most "on the carpet" at the time of his writing. And in handling a particular metaphysics, he follows the inspiration of his own nature and his own genius; he opposes the general idea not to another, contradictory, general idea, but to specific, individual, concrete facts.

Voltaire has a very strong sense of the real, and to him the existence of evil is a fact constantly observable in our human existence. Irrespective of metaphysical principles of good and evil, of liberty and determination, there is definite, concrete evil in the world, and despite the centuries of metaphysical and theological speculation, mankind has not fully reconciled the omnipotence and goodness of God with individual, specific, present, shocking, horrible evils. Philosophical principles may reconcile the mind to what seems to us a contradiction on the abstract level, but they cannot really satisfy us and quiet the questionings of heart and mind when a youngster is burned to death because he returned to his flaming home to save a baby still inside, or when a murdered child's body is found violated and horribly abused by a maniac, or when hundreds of thousands of people are systematically exterminated in gas chambers.

These things do indeed happen, but they are fortunately not matters of common experience; we do not like to think of them, and consequently we do not think of them very often. We like to consider, as did Voltaire in his earlier writings, that these evils are, after all, not very usual, and that they are far outweighed by the good which we find more frequently in life. This, of course, is no answer at all to the intellectual problem, but it is a little bit of balm for the emotions. Since it is no answer, however, the question itself remains with all its power to disquiet, ready to force itself again upon us when we witness some new horror.

As Voltaire grew older (he was about sixty-five when he wrote *Candide* in 1758 or 1759), he became more and more inclined toward a pessimistic view of the human scene, and consequently more and more strongly opposed to the popular "optimistic" philosophy current at the time. And then, on November 1, 1755, Nature's own version of the atomic bomb hit the city of Lisbon; the immediate physical and psychological effects of the frightful earthquake of All Saints' Day were indeed very like those which followed the catastrophe of Hiroshima: virtually complete material wreckage of a prosperous, populous city, some thirty thousand people killed, tremendous property damage, and worldwide horror, fright and dismay. The only essential difference is that then it was the blind forces of external nature which produced the cataclysm and the terror, whereas today it is the blind forces of human nature which produce the cataclysm and inspire the same terror.

The Christian of today, like the Christian of 1755, can only say that such horrors are undoubtedly and clearly evil, and that God is undoubtedly and clearly omnipotent, wise and good; we do not, our finite human minds cannot, adequately understand the relation between these two propositions. Voltaire, who was no Christian, answered, however, like the Christian, that we do not understand; but he did not add the second proposition. He believed in the existence of God, indeed, but apparently conceived of Him as a sort of Aristotelian "unmoved mover" or a Cartesian Creator who builds His world-machine and then lets it run without further interference. For, as we have seen, Voltaire's "we do not understand" is a far more general negation than that of the Christian mind confronted by the problem of evil. Like his hero, Candide, he believes that we cannot grapple with any basic truths at all, and any attempt to do so leads not only into error, but necessarily into preposterous and ridiculous affirmations.

At this point, of course, Voltaire really comes into his own, for he is the supreme master of the great art of ridicule, which is a special and frequently a very salubrious gift of the French nation. No matter how much we may disapprove, or how much we may be shocked by *Candide,* it would be difficult indeed to read it without a smile and many a chuckle. For Voltaire had a sharp eye and an even sharper tongue. Costumes and customs may have changed since 1759, but we can still recognize his characters among our contemporaries: the pompousness, the obstinacy, the unthinking cruelty, the cynicism of his rapidly and summarily sketched caricatures strike home, for they are all about us, and we are fortunate indeed if they are not also all within us.

But once our imaginations and our memories have been amused, and our sense of the incongruous has been tickled by his feathery pen, and after our indignation has been aroused, as he intended, by some of the dreadful abuses he holds up to our view, we may lay down the book and wonder what it all adds up to. Voltaire's own conclusion is, of course, clearly indicated

in the text: the world is full of misfortune, suffering and wickedness which we cannot understand and against which we cannot
possibly protect ourselves completely. The only sensible thing
to do, therefore, is to "cultivate our own garden." In other
words, we must abandon any attempt to understand our existence and to lead a reasoned life based on reasoned principles;
we must simply take refuge in activity which will occupy our
minds and provide our material requirements, and thus avoid
the three great evils of boredom, vice and need.

Voltaire, we know, was a reader of, and naturally an opponent
of, Pascal. They were both men of unusually sharp vision, extreme sensitivity and great genius, and they were both preoccupied with the same fundamental problem of man's misery
as he finds himself adrift in an apparently senseless, hostile and
(if we think too much about it) intolerable world. That is why,
Pascal said, we cannot bear to be alone; we simply cannot face
our thoughts and ourselves. Hence our eternal need of activity
and distraction. But these can never satisfy either our minds or
our souls; they are merely temporary palliatives.

Pascal, of course, found firm support for his mind, answers
to his intellectual questionings, and strength for his soul in the
revealed doctrine and supernatural aids of Christian religion.
Voltaire, on the other hand, as we see in *Candide,* resolutely, if
tacitly, rejected such a fundamental solution, and simply took
refuge in Pascal's distraction, for, from the point of view of the
philosophical and psychological problems presented by human
and natural evil in the world, his cultivation of his garden is
merely a form of withdrawal and a useful distraction.

It is easy to yield to Voltaire's wit and his "wisdom." To do
so makes it possible for us to relish the first to the fullest and to
feel a self-satisfied glow in that we are enlightened enough to
share in the second. Even so zealous a Catholic as Alfred Noyes,
in his really extraordinary book on Voltaire, is so far misled
by chosen passages of his writings and gestures in his life, as well
as by some of the sound things he says and some of his real
virtues, that he comes to believe and stoutly maintain that
Voltaire was a "good" Christian; he even suggests, *mirabile dictu,*
that he may one day be canonized, and that that may be a very
fine thing!

This is simply to ignore the fact that Voltaire was the sworn enemy not only of the Catholic Church but of all revealed and organized religion. His famous cry, *Écrasez l'Infame* ("Crush the Infamous One"), is directed not merely against the abuses of religion which he satirizes in *Candide* and in almost all his other works, but against all supernatural religion itself. His God—for he believed, or claimed to believe, in God—was a philosophical necessity to account for the presence of order in the world, and a moral necessity to guarantee the preservation of social order in the same world. That is, of course, what he meant by his famous "If God didn't exist, He would have to be invented."

Voltaire's "God," then, is a combination of the God of Aristotle and the God of Karl Marx; He is at once the Prime Mover and the Opiate of the People. He is not at all, as Pascal would have said, the God of Abraham, Isaac and Jacob, but merely the God of the philosophers and the God of the capitalists Who serves only to keep the down-trodden proletariat in its chains. And Voltaire, by the way, was a successful capitalist who lived in ease and luxury from the proceeds of his profitable speculations and investments.

If it is easy to let oneself be beguiled by Voltaire's brilliant wit, or be inspired to admiration by his amusing and unerring exposure of human frailties and imbecilities and his sincere indignation at human intolerance and cruelty, it is equally easy to condemn the unholy mocker. However, it is perhaps the part of prudence and justice, as well as of charity, to consider the thoughts as objectively and as critically as need be, and leave the thinker to his only qualified Judge.

This is not to proclaim his rightness but merely to point out that he lived in a period when he beheld all too frequently a most disedifying spectacle of moneylenders in the Temple, of bigotry in the name of truth and of cruelty in the name of love. And it may perhaps be presumptuous to affirm too boldly that, in his place, we should have had a greater firmness of faith and depth of spiritual vision.

JEAN MISRAHI

SELECTED BIBLIOGRAPHY

TORREY, Norman L., *The Spirit of Voltaire*. Columbia University Press.
WADE, Ira O., *Studies on Voltaire*. Princeton University Press.
MORIZE, André, ed. *Voltaire, Candide*. Société des Textes Français Modernes.
HAVENS, George R., ed. *Selections from Voltaire*. Appleton-Century-Crofts.
VOLTAIRE, François-Marie, *Candide*. Random House (Modern Library).
VOLTAIRE, François-Marie, *Candide*. Regnery.

Lavoisier: Elements of Chemistry, *Part I*

ANTOINE-LAURENT LAVOISIER was born and baptized in Paris on August 26, 1743, as attested by the registers of the *paroisse Saint-Merry*. His father was a lawyer, and his mother came from a legal family. A student at the renowned *Collège Mazarin,* he at first wished to follow in his father's footsteps in the law. Soon, however, the inclination toward the natural sciences grew very strong in him, and it was nurtured by his teachers: Jussieu, the botanist; La Caille, the mathematician; Guettard, the mineralogist, and Rouelle, the chemist. His philosophical training was influenced by the teachings of the Abbé de Condillac. Because of his father's and mother's wealth, Lavoisier was never obliged to learn a gainful trade and was free to yield to his scientific bent. He is thus among the last of those great gifted amateurs who, in the course of the seventeenth and eighteenth centuries, devoted an independent income to the cultivation of the sciences.

His first publications were presented to the Paris Academy of Sciences about 1764. In 1767 he became chemical assistant to Guettard in the preparation of a mineralogical atlas of France. His first chemical analyses already show the logical clarity and the physical precision that were to characterize all his work. Lavoisier was one of the first chemists to make use of the balance, and to weigh his materials before and after a chemical change. He was thus able to banish from chemistry the hypothetical principle of combustion, phlogiston, which did not obey the laws of gravity, and to establish the Law of Conservation of Mass which he put succinctly: *Rien ne se perd, rien ne se crée* ("Nothing is lost, nothing is created"). He may be considered a direct founder of Quantitative Analysis, that branch of chemistry upon which rests our knowledge of the composition of substances, which we represent today by compact shorthand formulae such as H_2O (for water) or $NaCl$ (for salt). His measurements of Heats of Combustion make him a forerunner of Physical Chemistry, which was not to be developed until a century later.

In 1768 Lavoisier became *membre-adjoint* of the Academy. In 1769, presumably to increase his income, he entered the corporation of the *Fermiers-généraux*, to whom the French Monarchy farmed out the unpopular job of collecting the taxes. His association with the Farmers-General developed his interest in economics, agriculture, taxation, finance, banking, etc., upon which subjects he wrote extensively.

In December, 1771, Lavoisier married the daughter of another *fermier-général:* Maria Paulze, who was then only 13 years old. They had no children. She became his faithful scientific assistant, drew copperplates for his publications, translated English chemical writings. She made the Lavoisier home a brilliant social gathering-point for all the scientific and intellectual life of Paris.

In 1774 Priestley discovered, by heating red calcined mercury (today called mercuric oxide), a new species of air or gas which he called "dephlogisticated air" (discovered independently in 1772 by Scheele, who called it "fire air"). In October, 1774, Priestley came to Paris and communicated his discovery at a dinner in Lavoisier's home. He explained that, in his dephlogisticated air, a candle would burn much more brilliantly than in ordinary air and, in it, a glowing splint would burst into flames. Lavoisier later on was to claim co-discovery of this air, together with Priestley and Scheele (*Elements of Chemistry*, p. 45 of the Regnery reprint). He was not strictly honest in this matter. He went on to study Priestley's air, showed it to be essential for the support of both life and combustion, to be the vital or respirable portion of ordinary atmospheric air, to be a constituent of many varied substances: water, metallic earths and calces, and acids. Lavoisier was the first to recognize the far-reaching importance of Priestley's dephlogisticated air in the organization of chemistry. He proposed, therefore, that it be given a simple name. Since the combustion of sulfur, phosphorus and charcoal in this air always gives rise to acids, to quote his own words:

we have given to the base [*i.e.*, to the substance] . . . of the respirable portion of atmospheric air, the name of *oxygen*, from ὄξυς, *acidum*, and γείνομαι, *gignor*, because one of the most general properties of this base is to form acids, by combining with many different substances.

From this simple name of oxygen, he was able to develop a systematic chemical nomenclature *(e.g., metallic calces and earths came to be known as metallic oxides)* which was formally presented to the Academy in 1787 in collaboration with Morveau, Berthollet and Fourcroy, and which has formed the basis of chemical nomenclature to the present day. Thus, while Lavoisier did not actually discover oxygen, he baptized it, so to speak, and from a study of its reactions he was able to systematize many of the previously confusing facts of chemistry. The detailed exposition of his system was brought together in the *Traité élémentaire de Chymie,* published in 1789. This book inaugurated a new period in chemical teaching and research.

In 1790 Lavoisier was appointed to the Weights and Measures Commission, which was to give to the world uniform measures in the metric system. In 1794 the former Farmers-General were placed under arrest by the Republican Government of France. Lavoisier at first thought to flee, but then let himself be made a prisoner in the hope of alleviating reprisals against his colleagues. He was convinced that he would be promptly exonerated. Instead, he was condemned to death by the *Tribunal révolutionnaire* on the charge, among others, of having put water in the soldiers' tobacco. When an appeal for clemency was made to the court on the grounds that he was also a famous chemist, the presiding judge is reported to have remarked: *La République n'a pas besoin de savants* ("The Republic needs no scientists"). This remark is believed by some to be apocryphal, but apocryphal or not, it well reveals the temper of the Era of Terror under the tyranny of Robespierre. On May 8, 1794, Lavoisier and his father-in-law were both guillotined.

This barbarous act provoked universal indignation. Robert Kerr, who translated the *Traité élémentaire* into English, writes in his translator's preface:

The Philosophical World has now infinitely to deplore the tragical and untimely death of the great Lavoisier; who has left a rare example of splendid talents and great wealth, at the same time immersed in numerous and important public employments, which he executed with diligent intelligence, and devoting his princely fortune and vast abilities to the sedulous cultivation and most successful improvement of the Sciences. If the sanguinary tyranny of the monster Robespierre had committed only that outrage against eternal Justice, a succeeding age of the most perfect government would scarcely have sufficed, to France and to the world, to repair the prodigious injury that loss has produced to chemistry, and to all the sciences and economical arts with which it is connected. (*Elements of Chemistry*, 3rd English Edition, pp. x-xi.)

The *Berlinische Jahrbuch der Pharmacie* for 1795 writes in its obituary:

In May, 1794, Chemistry lost one of her most renowned favorites in Mr. Lavoisier. He was guillotined under the frightful despotism of Robespierre, after conviction by the Revolutionary Tribunal in Paris as a former Farmer-General. It would be right to take this opportunity to curse that abominable tyrant, who has disgraced humanity even in the case of the celebrated Lavoisier, and through him also, has increased the number of those unfortunates, in whose blood he has bathed his ambition.

Robespierre did not survive this "triumph" long, as he was himself guillotined on July 28, 1794.

Lavoisier's personal motto, *Signabitque viam flammis*, describes the tenor of his life. The catholicity of his interests, his numerous writings on economic subjects, make him a forerunner of the social and political sciences. Yet, it is in the domain of the natural sciences, and particularly in chemistry, that his fame is securely established. True to his motto, his chemical work did cast a flame that enlightened the path of· chemical research for succeeding generations and led chemistry through its fantastic and phenomenal growth of a century and a half to our own tragic days of the atomic bomb.

In his *Elements of Chemistry* Lavoisier enunciated some of those valid principles of scientific research and teaching which have ever served as a guide to those who cultivate the natural sciences:

I have imposed upon myself, as a law, never to advance but from what is known to what is unknown; never to form any conclusion which is not an immediate consequence necessarily flowing from observation and experiment; and always to arrange the facts, and the conclusions which are drawn from them, in such an order as shall render it most easy for beginners in the study of chemistry thoroughly to understand them.

The rigorous law from which I have never deviated, of forming no conclusions which are not fully warranted by experiment, and of never supplying the absence of facts, has prevented me from comprehending in this work the branch of chemistry which treats of affinities. . . . The principal data [of affinities] are still wanting.

That is to say, the data for writing satisfactory chemical formulae are still wanting, so Lavoisier refrains from writing any of them. Let us see what he thinks about the notion of *elements:*

. . . the fondness for reducing all the bodies in nature to three or four elements, proceeds from a prejudice which has descended to us from the Greek Philosophers. The notion of four elements, which, by the variety of their proportions, compose all the known substances in nature, is a mere hypothesis, assumed long before the first principles of experimental philosophy or of chemistry had any existence.

. . . if, by the term *elements,* we mean to express those simple and indivisible atoms of which matter is composed, it is extremely probable we know nothing at all about them; but if we apply the term *elements* or *principles of bodies,* to express our idea of the last point which analysis is capable of reaching, we must admit, as elements, all the substances into which we are able to reduce bodies by decomposition.

The scientific caution used by Lavoisier in the above definition of the word *element* is all the more remarkable when we consider how the twentieth century has been using radioactivity to smash the "atoms" of the nineteenth century's "elements." Let us continue with Lavoisier's words:

Chemistry affords two general methods of determining the constituent principles of bodies, the method of analysis, and that of synthesis. When, for instance, by combining water with alcohol, we form the species of liquor called . . . brandy . . . we certainly have a right to conclude, that brandy . . . is composed of alcohol combined with water; and in general it ought to be considered as a principle in chemical science, never to rest satisfied without both these species of proofs.

. . . the choice of our evidences is of far greater consequence than their number.

In performing experiments, it is a necessary principle, which ought never to be deviated from, that they be simplified as much as possible, and that every circumstance capable of rendering their results complicated be carefully removed.

. . . in physics, and in chemistry, it is not allowable to suppose what is capable of being ascertained by direct experiment. . . .

The *Traité élémentaire de Chymie* appeared in 1789, and was promptly translated into English as *The Elements of Chemistry,* by Robert Kerr, of the Royal College of Surgeons and of the Royal Physical Society of Edinburgh. This translation proved so popular that a third edition was already appearing in 1796. The book is divided into an Author's Preface, three Parts, and thirteen Appendices. Part I deals with the composition of the atmosphere, combustion and the formation of acids; Part II, with the combination of acids and bases and the formation of neutral salts; Part III, with the instruments and operations of chemistry. This book does not attempt to be a literary or metaphysical work —it illustrates only too well the "divorce" between philosophy and science, which is one of the tragedies of modern man. It is strictly a technical work, and as such does not make easy reading. It is clearly written, however, and the most involved arguments can always be followed to their logical conclusions. A reprint of the Preface and Part I, published by Regnery in 1949, makes this work available to modern readers but is unfortunately obscured by a number of textual inaccuracies and omissions.

Lavoisier lived at a troubled time, which marked a turning point in the history of science and in the history of mankind. *La grande Révolution,* which put Lavoisier to death because it had no need of scientists, was to offer a prize to Nicolas Leblanc for setting up the first chemical factory for the synthesis of soda from salt. Science soon was to step out of the ivory tower where she had been cultivated by the devotion and income of gifted amateurs: Newton, Leibnitz, Pascal, Descartes, Priestley, Cavendish, Lavoisier. She was about to invade the market place with the soda industry and to enter into the councils of war with Napoleon's scientific advisers. She was to enter upon a period of unprecedented growth and expansion, in which her devotees were to earn their income from her, whether through teaching, industry or governmental subsidy.

Our present time is also a troubled time, and again seems to be a turning point for science and for mankind. The crucial scientific problem—and the human problem—of today is to learn to live and to die in the apocalyptic vision of man, who has mastered the secret of nuclear energy, and has used it to kill or injure up to 140,000 citizens of Hiroshima at one single blow. In this sobering vision, we may draw inspiration from Lavoisier, who, in life, devoted his intelligence to the pursuit of knowledge and his talents to the service of his country, and who, in death, courageously did not forsake his colleagues in their hour of darkness.

ANDRÉ J. de BÉTHUNE

SELECTED BIBLIOGRAPHY

LAVOISIER, Antoine Laurent, *Elements of Chemistry*, translated by Robert Kerr. Third English edition, 1796. Edinburgh: William Creech.
BUGGE, Gunther, *Das Buch der Grossen Chemiker*. 1929. Berlin: Verlag Chemie.
MOORE, F. J., *A History of Chemistry*. Third edition, revised by William T. Hall. McGraw-Hill.
GLASSTONE, Samuel, *et al.*, *The Effects of Atomic Weapons*, 1950. Washington: U. S. Superintendent of Documents.
LAVOISIER, Antoine Laurent, *Elements of Chemistry, Book I*. 1949. Chicago: Regnery.

Gibbon: The Decline and Fall of the
Roman Empire, *Chapters 15 and 16*

THE SCENE is laid at Lausanne, Switzerland, between the hours of eleven and twelve on the night of June 27, 1787. The air is temperate, the sky serene, the silver orb of the moon is reflected on the waters of Lake Leman. All nature is silent. In a summerhouse on the shore above the Lake, a man who has been writing industriously, suddenly lays down the pen. The massive top-heavy head with its button nose and vast cheeks and chins is deeply creased with a shrewd smile, as of one conscious of having laid the foundations of lasting fame. With difficulty he raises his short and extraordinarily rotund body and slowly but eagerly takes several turns in a covered walk of acacias. His attitude is a mixture of vanity and pomposity, and in the semidarkness it appears that he is dressed in his inevitable flowered velvet. When he takes his seat again, the moment of elation has passed. He looks pensively at the pages just penned and seems more absorbed in the thought of the brevity of life than in the sweetness of fame. Despite the ridiculous body, this little man gives the impression of great mental power. Who is he? Is his conviction of enduring fame well founded?

Edward Gibbon (1737-1794) is the greatest historian not merely of the eighteenth century but of the English-speaking world. His masterpiece, *The Decline and Fall of the Roman Empire,* has taken permanent rank as a classic, by reason not only of its form but also of its substance. In it, Gibbon studied the fortunes of imperial Rome from the second to the fifteenth century. Dealing with a subject of great inherent interest, he produced a history which merits praise for "the inexhaustible labor employed on it, the immense condensation of matter, the luminous arrangement and general accuracy." No one before him had painted such a gigantic historical canvas. No one since his time has surpassed his art and irony. Gibbon's feeling of elation that night was fully justified. The masterpiece, which this moderately wealthy son of an English squire began to write while a member of Parliament, was destined to assure his fame. It is an unassailable glory of English letters.

Gibbon's candor must strike every reader of his *Autobiography*. He makes no attempt to strike heroic attitudes. He spares none of the foibles of which he is conscious: his love of comfort, his rather self-centered passion for reading, his desire for plenty of money and a place in congenial society. He frankly confesses his lack of ardor in love, religion and politics.

Devoid of large humanity and noble generosity, Gibbon did have redeeming qualities of heart. His personal affections for relatives and friends were strong and constant. And he had a certain grandeur of soul. The great ironist and investigator is not cool when he contemplates the art and language of Athens, the free polity of Rome or the dawning of the Renaissance. He reverences greatness when he sees it in St. Athanasius as well as in Marcus Aurelius.

Gibbon's self-knowledge and perseverance deserve respect. He made up his mind to achieve a monumental work, and he labored at it in spite of difficulties for fifteen years—no vulgar accomplishment, surely.

Unfortunately, Gibbon's masterpiece is dominated by a contempt for the Christian religion. As a young man he had accepted the position that the truth of Christianity has been attested to by the constant occurrence of physical and moral miracles, at least in the first five centuries of its existence. His reading led him to identify the truth of Christianity with Catholic dogma as it has been progressively formulated. This led to his premature conversion.

Attempts to lead him back to Protestantism, together with further reading, gave Gibbon the conviction that Christianity had never been guaranteed by miracles. Then a deep-seated antagonism to religion took hold of him. The history of Rome came to be for him the story of the triumph of barbarism and religion. As soon as Christianity was accorded recognition, it began, Gibbon thought, to create dissension throughout the empire, throwing province against province and class against class through the controversies and persecutions which disgraced it. A difference of opinion regarding the date of Easter grew in intensity. In time it became, in Gibbon's opinion, a major factor in the separation of Western and Eastern Christendom. This and other futile controversies seemed to Gibbon to have consumed the vitals of the empire. The role of Christianity was preeminently that of a disruptive agent.

Gibbon condemns no trait of the religion he despises so severely as he does its "bigotry." Christianity destroyed the traditional tolerance of the ancient world. What especially exasperated the great historian was that the several divisions of Christianity always reserved their sharpest weapons for each other. They were prone to engage in mortal combat over differences almost invisible to the nicest theological eye, reserving the right to adopt the reprobated opinion after blood had been shed.

Of all Christians, the monks, in Gibbon's opinion, were the most fanatical. Arising in Egypt, the fruitful mother of superstitions, they soon "overspread and darkened the face of the Christian world." Their swarms, legions, myriads, multitudes, millions *(sic)* were entirely lost to the defense of an empire which sadly needed able-bodied soldiers. For Gibbon, the monks were "incapable of fear, reason, or humanity." Against priesthood of every form and type, Gibbon had an incurable animus. The clergy of the East, he found incredibly disputatious. Their Western counterparts devoted more attention to practical affairs, acquiring wealth for themselves and power for their Church.

Gibbon's attitude to religion was generally sceptical. To Christianity and Judaism he was frankly hostile, and he considered the Roman Church in particular a perpetual foe of reason. In regard to Mohammedanism and paganism he was more indulgent. Indeed, more than any other character in the *Decline and Fall,* Julian the Apostate is Gibbon's hero.

Gibbon's mind can be seen in his masterpiece, which is at once gigantic and methodical, meticulous and animated. Among the works of applied literature, it has in matter of clarity, scope, density and excellence no rival in its time and age.

The modern concept of history written on a grand scale is that it should be meticulously accurate in fact and sound in interpretation, that it should illustrate and prove some tendency or principle shaping the destiny of society.

On the plane of fact, Gibbon has been enlarged, rectified or superseded at a hundred points. He used the sources which were to his hand, but much new material has come to light. His account of Mahomet is based on a discredited source. His description of the Byzantine empire is distorted, because he did not have access to Slavonic sources. His mistakes about the Middle Ages reflect the ignorance of his time, and in dealing with ecclesiastics he leans to the stories of their enemies and strives to discredit their own statements. But it is commonly agreed that as a matter of science, much of the *Decline and Fall,* especially in its early volumes, stands fast. "Whatever is read," says Freeman, "Gibbon must be read." "If," writes Bury, "we take into account the vast range of his work, his accuracy is amazing, and, with all his disadvantages, his slips are singularly few."

As for his comprehension of the destiny of society, Gibbon may have been a *philosophe,* but he was not a philosopher. He apparently thought that abstract reasoning was a waste of time. The theme of his masterpiece is the cause of the decline of the arts and virtue, of the fall of civilization and of the triumph of barbarism and religion. He rebuts the Christian view that the progress of human events is designed to aid the spread of the Church. His thesis is that Christianity hastened the fall of the empire by substituting faith for intelligence, fanaticism for patriotism and the Church for the state.

Gibbon's critical and ironical temper, as well as his subject, prevents him from accepting the theory of human progress as the key of history. Nor does he agree with Rousseau's opinion that human history is the story of a decline from a golden age of primitive simplicity. His view is the obvious one that man has advanced from the state of savagery and can never wholly relapse into that state.

To the support of this vague principle, Gibbon brings his rather shadowy deism with a faint hope of immortality. He cherished a genuine respect for the pure, benevolent and simple maxims of the Gospel but finds them overlaid in the churches with asceticism and worldly ecclesiasticism. He fails to comprehend the spirit responsible for the development of dogma. All is perverse and savage arrogance of intellect and party spirit.

That is why he brings his critical and ironical spirit to bear on historical Christianity.

Gibbon's style has not always found favor. It repelled the critics of the Romantic movement. In their judgment the prim, complacent attitude of the eighteenth century was perfectly symbolized in the periods and mass of Gibbon. Clarity founded on the exclusion of all above the horizon and beneath the soil meant little to them. Charles Lamb thought that Gibbon's six fat, square volumes were books which are not books, which no gentleman would be caught reading. For Coleridge, Gibbon's style was detestable, and when he read a chapter in the *Decline and Fall* he seemed to be looking through a luminous haze in which the figures were all larger than life or distorted and discolored. He thought, too, that Gibbon had misstated and mistaken the character and influence of Christianity in a way which even an avowed infidel or atheist could not have done.

The majority of critics, however, and the best have seen in Gibbon's style "a thing of beauty and a joy forever." Hilaire Belloc, who detests Gibbon and has brought to the defense of Christianity as perfect a style as that which Gibbon used against it, calls the *Decline and Fall* far and away the most readable book in the English language. For this well-qualified judge there is not a dull line—certainly not a dull page—in the enormous work. Gibbon's prose has a strong rhythmic flow and a clear method. It has no equal for conciseness and exactitude of expression. Never has a man written a page of Tacitus and never, in Belloc's opinion, will a page be written in the manner of Gibbon. Lytton Strachey is also enthusiastic. For him, Gibbon's vital and penetrating imagination and his supreme capacity for general conceptions expressed themselves instinctively in an appropriate form. His work had classical lucidity, balance and precision to perfection.

Moreover, Gibbon had that sense of order which is so often lacking in productions of the mind and which enabled him to put system into the enormous chaos of materials which even in the eighteenth century faced the historian of Rome. In Strachey's judgment, Gibbon's superb constructive vision and astonishing facility in manipulating facts enabled him to drive a straight and narrow road through the unexplored wilderness of Roman history. Readers are invited to follow with easy pleasure along this marvelous highway, but they are not to stop or wander about. For Strachey, too, Gibbon's style is most exclusive. It rules out a multitude of human interests. There is no redundancy to fog the mind, no omission to confuse it. Gibbon's books have the supreme quality of excellent literature, namely, that it marches directly toward its end and attains it. His work, indeed, is primarily of value not as a record of his personality, which was cold and shifty, but for the style, and as a record of a great historical mind. It is a splendid exhibition of a great task well done.

Chapters 15 and 16 of the *Decline and Fall* have been chosen for special consideration here because they represent Gibbon's preface and introduction to his treatment of Christianity as a disruptive force. They are so distinctive, indeed, that they have, in recent years, been issued in cheap reprints in the interests of militant rationalism. In this form these chapters have reached literally millions of readers. We shall formulate brief summaries of these two chapters in illustration of the criticism already given.

In Chapter 15 Gibbon studies the means by which the Christian faith attained to supremacy over the established religions of the Roman empire. At the start he professes in his sly way that "an obvious but satisfactory answer could be found in the convincing evidence of Christian doctrine and in the ruling Providence of its Author." But he thinks that Providence wisely uses the passions of the human heart and the general circumstances of mankind to execute its purposes. So, secondary causes of the rapid growth of the Christian Church are sought. These, Gibbon finds, are five: 1) the intolerance of the early Christians; 2) the doctrine of a future state; 3) the claim to miraculous power; 4) the sober and domestic virtues of the Christians and 5) their ecclesiastical organization.

Ever aiming to illuminate rather than to be comprehensive, Gibbon summarily examines the intolerance of the early Christians. Divine favor and a pure worship were offered to all as a gift but also as an obligation. This was, in his mind, a weapon borrowed from Judaism, but the Christians manipulated it with more dexterity than the Jews had shown. Indeed, in the early days Christian exclusivism was not so stern as to bar the practice of Judaism or the profession of Gnosticism. But Jews and Gnostics as well as Christians held that the demons were the authors, patrons and objects of pagan idolatry. The most trifling mark of respect to the national worship of the pagans was considered direct homage yielded to Satan. As these rites were practiced in every circumstance of business and pleasure, and of public and private life, the Christian always had an occasion for declaring and confirming his opposition to them. In this manner was developed an invincible valor which disdained capitulation and was resolved to win.

Gibbon sees in the Christian doctrine of a future state an effective weapon, because neither the philosophy nor religion of the time offered to the careless polytheist any protection against it. Christianity promised him, at least in the beginning, a thousand years of happiness in this world at the end of the present order, which was conceived as being at hand, and everlasting happiness in a better life. If he did not accept, then there was the menace of eternal torture. If the pagan could "once persuade himself to suspect that the Christian religion might be true," the safest and most prudent thing was to become a Christian.

Gibbon makes very clear that he considers the Christian claim to miraculous power to have been merely a claim. But still, it was somehow a potent weapon, because the primitive Christians were ever ready to believe the most extraordinary things, and the curious and credulous pagans displayed an unresisting softness of temper by meekly entering the society which falsely claimed miraculous powers.

In his treatment of the sober and domestic virtues of the Christians, Gibbon fails to make clear how they furnished the Church with a formidable weapon. According to his view, Christianity lured into its bosom the most atrocious criminals, who thereupon devoted themselves to penance. Moreover, once become Christians, they were possessed by a great desire of supporting the reputation of the society they had entered. This enabled the Fathers to preach a doctrine of extreme rigorism, condemning all the pleasures and activities which nature loves. Gibbon makes no attempt to explain how such a stern code won the hardened pagan heart. Probably he considered these virtues in relation to his fifth cause: organization.

Barred by their puritanical rigorism from the joys and honors of learning, fortune, society and war, the primitive Christians put all their energies into the Church. This led to the evolution in the third century of the monarchical episcopate, which, laying aside the language of exhortation, began to use that of command. It also produced the specifically Christian distinction between the clergy and laity. But what, Gibbon asks himself, was the secret of episcopal power at a time when the office was devoid of any temporal power? He finds it in the wealth which the Church early acquired by leading saintly parents to impoverish their children for the benefit of the bishops. Another cause was the dread power of excommunication, which would make the susceptible Christians believe themselves outcast in time and eternity. This close-knit organization united, Gibbon thought, the courage of the Christians and directed their aims, while it gave their efforts that irresistible weight which always accrues to a small band of well-trained and intrepid volunteers against the undisciplined multitude.

As if he were aware that his five reasons do not explain much, Gibbon, before ending the chapter, proceeds to give other reasons. He dwells on the weakness of paganism, with its anemic priesthood, and its vague and uncertain religious sentiments against the rampant incredulity and scepticism of the times. The surprising thing is, Gibbon muses, that Christianity did not spread even more rapidly than it did. It does not occur to him, apparently, that the rampant incredulity and scepticism might have been applied to Christianity.

Gibbon also speaks of the advantages Christianity derived from the conquest by Rome of the most civilized provinces of Europe, Asia and Africa, which served one sovereign and were united by the most intimate ties of laws, manners and religions. With Greek and Latin, Gibbon opines, the Church could teach all the peoples of the empire, except the peasants of Syria and Egypt. And the famed Roman roads opened the way for the heralds of the Gospel.

Gibbon finishes the fifteenth chapter with a rapid and, according to present-day standards, a very inadequate survey of the diffusion of Christianity during the first three centuries. He finds that, at most, a twentieth part of the subjects of the empire had, before Constantine, enlisted themselves under the banner of the cross. He also dwells with complacence on the thought that none of the really great men of the period became Christians.

The sixteenth chapter is less general in scope and will detain us but briefly. The causes, extent, duration and circumstance of the early persecutions of the Christian Church are investigated. Gibbon begins by enlarging on the tolerance and generosity of the imperial authorities in religious affairs. Despite their unsocial attitude and bloody rebellions, the Jews were always treated with consideration. Of course, the Christians did not form a nation as the Jews did, and they rejected the gods of Rome, of the empire and of all mankind. Again, the idea of the divinity professed in Christian circles was so pure and sublime that it failed to impress the pagan multitude, according to whose gross conceptions the Christians were atheists or, at best, worshipers of an obscure teacher whose equivocal birth, wandering life and ignominious death were far from impressive.

Moreover, the authorities were alarmed by the numbers and *esprit de corps* of organized Christianity. Its members, who obviously preferred its cult to family and nation, were to be found in every province and in nearly every city of the empire. The secrecy, too, in which Christian services were shrouded gave rise to charges of hidden abominations. These charges gained more ready credence because the mutual recriminations of the Christian factions lent them a certain measure of probability.

The heart of this chapter is a plaidoyer for the emperors who persecuted the Church. Gibbon argues that many decades elapsed before they considered the new sect worthy of their attention. Even when their hand was forced, they were cautious and reluctant in condemning. Punishments were moderate and the Church enjoyed long periods of peace. Gibbon dwells with complacency on the thought that the convicted Christian had only to cast a few grains of incense on an altar to merit pardon and praise. He dilates on the polished manners and liberal education of the judges who condemned the Christians. He shows that it was easy for them to escape death even without apostasy. He thinks that the transient persecutions really served to revive the zeal and restore the discipline of the Christians.

In the following pages Gibbon rapidly and inadequately reviews the early persecutions and hastens on to that of Diocletian.

His theme in these paragraphs is the relatively small number of those who suffered death at a time when the Christians were numerous and their foes exasperated. Not more than two thousand, he believes, were executed. And Gibbon excuses even this holocaust by reflecting on the far greater numbers of Christians slain by other Christians. The thought that the Church of Rome has defended by violence and massacres as well as by decrees of the Holy Office the position it obtained by fraud enables him to look with equanimity on the fate of the early Christians.

The factual content of these two chapters may have been competent in Gibbon's day; now it is definitely out of date. Gibbon lived before serious study of the numbers of the early Christians, and his idea of the course of the persecutions is quite jejune. But with this slight factual ballast and his delicate weapon of aloof, almost indifferent, mockery, Gibbon dealt Christianity a telling blow. All in all, he has fully merited his place in the *Index librorum prohibitorum* and the withering condemnation on the mystical plane by Cardinal Newman, who characterized Gibbon as "a cold heart, an impure mind and a scoffing spirit."

EDWARD A. RYAN

SELECTED BIBLIOGRAPHY

McCLOY, S. T., *Gibbon's Antagonism to Christianity*. Chapel Hill.
MORISON, J. A. Cotter, *Gibbon*. Macmillan.
STEPHEN, L., *History of English Thought in the Eighteenth Century*, Vol. I, pp. 446-457. Putnam.
BELLOC, Hilaire, *A Conversation with an Angel and Other Essays*, pp. 129-137. Harper.
STRACHEY, Lytton, *Portraits in Miniature*, pp. 152-165. Harcourt.
GIBBON, Edward, *The Decline and Fall of the Roman Empire*. Random House (Modern Library).
GIBBON, Edward, *The Decline and Fall of the Roman Empire*. Regnery.

Mill: On Liberty

THIS 100-PAGE ESSAY [1] deals with "civil, or social liberty: the nature and the limits which can be legitimately exercised by society over the individual." It is generally recognized as the most careful and studied expression of J. S. Mill's political thought. In this judgment Mill himself would probably concur, for he writes in his *Autobiography:*

The *Liberty* is likely to survive longer than anything else that I have written . . . because it (is) a kind of philosophic text-book on a single truth, which the changes progressively taking place in modern society tend to bring out into ever stronger relief: the importance, to man and to society, of a large variety of types of character, and of giving full freedom to human nature to expand itself in innumerable and conflicting directions.[2] (New York: Columbia Univ. Press, 1924, p. 177.)

At any rate, *On Liberty* is no doubt Mill's most typical, characteristic work. Through its pages breathes the same brave idealism which stamped the whole of Mill's life; the same reformist zeal which so often made him throw logic to the wind; the same crusading belief in the ever-ascending progress of humanity under the banner of Utilitarianism.

From his early years J. S. Mill was brought up to be an apostle of Utilitarian ideals. Logically, the *principle of utility* ("the greatest happiness for the greatest number") led to the belief that democracy, as the rule of the majority, was the only panacea for all social injustice and tyranny. Tyranny, the elder Utilitarians said, is possible only when the government is in the hands of one or of a few; not when it is in the hands of the many, that is, of the people themselves. For, in that case, the rulers will be identified with the ruled; and the rulers would not wish to enslave themselves.

And so, in Mill's youth the Utilitarian crusade was directed against privilege, against the so-called "sinister interests of the few." The way to social happiness was to abolish privilege, to do away with "rotten-boroughs," to reform municipalities, to pass a new Poor Law: in general, to overhaul the machinery of government in order to make it more responsive and responsible to the will of the people. The Utilitarians got what they wanted. The Reform Bill of 1832 was passed, the government machinery was overhauled, power shifted from an oligarchy to a democracy: but, alas, the Utilitarian promise of greater social happiness did not materialize. And the people, instead of wanting less inter- ference on the part of government, wanted more.

Thus, in 1859, when he wrote *On Liberty*, Mill was forced to admit his disillusionment:

In political and philosophical theories as well as in persons, success discloses faults and infirmities which failure might have concealed from observation. The notion that the people have no need to limit their power over themselves, might seem axiomatic when popular government was a thing only dreamed about or read of as having existed at some distant period in the past . . . [but in reality] such phrases as "self-government" and the "power of the people over themselves," do not state the true state of the case. The "people" who exercise power are not always the same people with those over whom it is exercised; and the "self-government" spoken of is not the gov- ernment of each by himself, but of each by all the rest.[3]

In other words, a change of government may only mean a change from the tyranny of one or of a few to the tyranny of the many. Hence, the problem of limiting the power of govern- ment over individuals loses none of its importance and urgency, even when those who wield the power are regularly accountable to the people, as they are in a democracy.

The purpose, then, of this essay is to find the principle which should govern and limit the interference of government with the individual by way of compulsion and control. There is noth- ing new or original about the areas of freedom which Mill wants to safeguard from all government interference. Freedom of thought, freedom of conscience, freedom of opinion and dis- cussion—these are very old topics indeed. That Mill was able to bring fresh interest into the matter is a tribute to his ability: to the crisp and forceful style, the high idealism, the boldness and novelty of reasoning, which he brought to play in the writing of this work.

And that is just the trouble: some of his premises are too idealistic, some of his arguments too bold, to be true. Let us take, for instance, his arguments for absolute freedom of opinion. No one would deny on general principles that man has a right to express his honest convictions and opinions freely; that the government has no right to control thought or opinion; that the more the people are taught to think and act for themselves the better for the people, and the better for the government. Free discussion is good and necessary in order to clarify issues, to reach by collective effort at the truth and to arrive at consensus.

But when Mill argues that discussion is good and must be stimulated, even when the issues are no longer debatable, just because the truth needs perpetual contradiction if it is to prove itself the truth and to remain a living truth, he would seem to overestimate the value of contradiction and disagreement, as if the only way to keep truth alive was to disagree with it; and he would seem to ask the impossible, namely, that man must challenge every belief until he has himself examined its ultimate foundation; that no man worth his salt is to accept any truth upon the authority of another. Clearly, this would be to advocate intellectual suicide. The wisest of us has to take nine tenths of his beliefs on trust, on reasonable faith.

Again, when Mill defends absolute freedom of thought on the grounds that in persecuting any belief whatsoever, we might perhaps be persecuting the truth, and by suppressing it, we might perhaps be depriving mankind of it for centuries to come—as happened, he says, in the case of the Lollards, the Hussites, the Albigensians and others—he would seem to contradict not only history but even himself.

He had just told us that the best thing that could happen to truth is to be contradicted, persecuted; for truth lives on contradiction and thrives under persecution. Now he is telling us that it was unfortunate that the Lollards, the Hussites, the Albigensians and others were persecuted, because these people had the truth, but the truth, alas, was suppressed. It would seem then that, survival or suppression, the other side always has the truth, as long as it is the Church who does the persecuting.

This is, to my mind, like playing both ends against the middle. It is a minor point, but I bring it up because, in this work and his other works, Mill, despite his genuine honesty and sincerity, is now and then betrayed by his old prejudice against the Church into historical inaccuracies and misrepresentations.

To come to the heart of Mill's thesis, let us examine the principle which he uses to establish the line of demarcation between government interference and individual freedom:

The sole end for which mankind are warranted, individually or collectively, in interfering with the liberty of action of any of their number, is self-protection. The only purpose for which power can be rightly exercised over any member of a civilized community, against his will, is to prevent harm to others.[4]

In the last two chapters of this essay, Mill applies this principle to specific problems of his day. Space does not permit us to discuss them singly and to point out where Mill might have been too narrow or too liberal in his concept of government interference. At any rate, it is not the concrete applications that we are really interested in. These are subject to infinite variations, which can only be discussed in the context of concrete facts and circumstances. What we are interested in here is Mill's principle itself. What should we think of it?

Clearly, Mill's principle of liberty is that of nineteenth-century individualistic liberalism. The only reason for government interference in society is *self-protection*, that is to say, to protect individuals against individuals, and individuals against society and vice-versa. This is essentially a negative function, like the function of a policeman or an umpire. It is not the function of a policeman to pass or to repeal laws for the common good. In an individualistic state, such as Mill postulates, there can be no common good to be attained by common effort; there can only be private goods to be procured by individuals as individuals under an agreement of *laissez faire*.

The whole social mechanism revolves around this principle. Leave us alone to work it out for ourselves, yes, even to fight it out among ourselves. Do not interfere with us, unless it be to pull us out of clinches, or to wave us to a neutral corner. In this kind of game, it is a question of the survival of the fittest: the rich become richer, the poor poorer.

But the time came when the poor could no longer endure their poverty; when, in the face of social injustice, they became convinced that, by pulling down the individualistic order of society, they had nothing to lose and everything to gain. The means they used to do this job was that same individualistic liberty which nineteenth-century liberalism regarded as the *summum bonum* of society. For liberty, when men act in bodies, is power, and when they act outside the law it is sheer power. Thus, by a strange irony of history, the liberalistic state which had no god but liberty was turned into a state which had no god but power. From an essentially atomistic society made up of individual wills and private ends, it became a monolithic totalitarian state whose motto is: "all in the state, nothing outside the state, nothing against the state." *Les extrèmes se touchent.*

Rousseau, Locke and their followers, it goes without saying, did not foresee nor intend this strange by-product from their individualistic theories. They were guilty of no greater crime than that of exaggerated idealism. They had too optimistic a notion of the individual. That, basically, was the whole trouble with Mill. He conceived society in the abstract, as composed of individuals, who seemingly cannot act wrongly, as long as they act freely. Hence the less government, the better. Such a principle enshrines, of course, some truth, but it is not a sacrosanct dogma to be preserved at all cost. Between the crazy idealism of Rousseau and the equally crazy pessimism of Hobbes, there is a third course—the sound realism of Burke.

On this point let me quote rather generously from Burke's *Reflections on the Revolution in France:*

Government is a contrivance of human wisdom to provide for human wants. Men have a right that these wants should be provided for by this wisdom. Among these wants is to be reckoned the want, out of civil society, of a sufficient restraint upon their passions. Society requires not only that the passions of individuals should be subjected, but that even in the mass and body, as well as in the individuals, the inclinations of men should frequently be thwarted, their will controlled, and their passions brought into subjection. This can only be done by a power out of themselves . . . but as the liberties and the restrictions vary with times and circumstances, and admit of infinite modifications, they cannot be settled upon any abstract rule; and nothing is so foolish as to discuss them upon that principle.[5]

If Mill had lived through the nineteenth century into the opening decades of the twentieth, when at last the economic slavery of the masses resulting from liberalism reached its bloody climax in the dictatorship of the proletariat and the rise of the Fascist state, he too, no doubt, would have taken Burke's wise and measured view on the uses of liberty and its relation to government. But it was achievement enough to have made his own generation deeply conscious of the central dilemma which faces all republican government. In Lincoln's words, "Must a government, of necessity, be too strong for the liberties of its own people, or too weak to maintain its own existence?"

Viewing liberty, as he did, as an absolute good, and government as, at best, a necessary evil, Mill saw no way out of the dilemma but by allowing the government no other function but that of guardian of law and order, while the springs of action and progress are solely to be provided by the unhampered freedom of individuality of the citizen. As there are to be no limits to freedom of thought and discussion, but what might be absolutely necessary to ward off "a clear and present danger," so there are to be no barriers whatsoever to individual action and initiative, but what might be absolutely necessary to safeguard personal rights from individual or collective interference. In society, as Mill conceived it, the individuals are the only reality; the state is nothing more than a free and rather arbitrary network of relations between individuals who have agreed to live together in order to promote their individual purposes and ends, as individuals. The state, then, has no objective reality and essence all its own, distinct from the collectivity; and the common good is no more than the sum-total of private goods.

Under these premises I do not see how Mill could salvage his highly prized freedom of individuality. For, if the state is nothing more than the collectivity, that is, the sum-total of individuals; if the common good is nothing more than the sum-total of private goods, then by the utilitarian principle of the greatest happiness for the greatest number, the freedom of the majority could very well be the oppression of the minority. I do not see how Mill could, in this supposition, say: "If all mankind minus one were of one opinion, and only one person were of the contrary opinion, mankind would be no more justified in silencing that one person, than he, if he had the power, would be justified in silencing mankind." [6]

Only in the sovereign concept of the common good can the rights of the minority be protected. Private good, because it is individual, individualizes, or rather divides society into its component individuals. While the common good is common precisely because it belongs to the community as a whole—to the majority as well at to the minority. This is so, because the common good is good for the human person as such. In the words of Jacques Maritain:

> The common good of the city is neither the mere collection of private goods, nor the proper good of a whole which, like the species with respect to its individuals or the hive with respect to its bees, relates the parts to itself alone and sacrifices them to itself. It is the good *human* life of the multitude, of a multitude of persons; it is their communion in good living. It is therefore common to both *the whole and the parts* into which it flows back and which, in turn, must benefit from it. [7]

By its very nature, then, the common good, which is the government's only *raison d'être,* cannot be destructive of genuine human good—hence, of genuine human freedom. On the contrary, the order of the common good, which at times may require that freedom be restricted if it is at all to be possessed, is freedom's proper climate and native home. For, to meet the test of the common good, the state cannot command anything that is, in the last analysis, destructive or restrictive of true human good, of the *bonum honestum* of the human person. As an individual, he may indeed be asked to sacrifice himself for the common good, but because he is no mere individual—that is, a part of the social whole—but also a person—that is, a spiritual whole in himself, a reality which, subsisting spiritually, constitutes under God a universe unto itself (as Maritain puts it)—man cannot be asked to sacrifice his transcendent destiny, nor indeed to sacrifice any true human good, unless the sacrifice is meant to benefit him ultimately as it benefits the social whole. Man, as a person, cannot be used as a means to an end. As a person, he is, under God, an end unto himself.

Not on the absolute independence of the individual, then, as Mill would have it, but on the transcendence of personality, is human liberty to be firmly rooted and made to grow. Only when it serves the true ends of the human person is liberty, in the words of Burke, "a good to be improved, and not an evil to be lessened . . . [so that] it ought to be the constant aim of every wise public counsel to find out by cautious experiments, and rational cool endeavors, with how little, not how much of restraint the community can subsist." [8]

In this essay *On Liberty* Mill reaches the same conclusion. That he started from the false premise of individualistic liberalism only proves that he was a child of his own generation; it does not take away from the real and lasting worth of his work. In our age, whose main obsession seems to be collective security, whether it be under a Communist regime, a Fascist dictatorship, or the paternalistic providence of the Welfare State, we need to realize what Mill so vividly realized: that security can be bought at too high a price; that when it is bought at the expense of liberty and personal initiative, it is no security at all, but base slavery; that, in the end, man's earthly salvation is not achieved by becoming a cog or wheel in a machine nor, to use Secretary Byrnes's phrase, by becoming "an economic slave pulling an oar in the galley of the State," but by developing all the hidden potentialities of man's spiritual being, under a regime which would allow as much play to human freedom as is compatible with the ends of a well-ordered Society.

PACIFICO A. ORTIZ

NOTES

1. The full essay is found in *Utilitarianism, Liberty, and Representative Government* by John Stuart Mill, New York: E. P. Dutton & Co. (Everyman's Library), pp. 61-170; quotations will be taken from this edition.
2. *Autobiography of J. S. Mill*, New York. Columbia University Press, 1924, p. 177.
3. *Utilitarianism, Liberty, and Representative Government*, p. 67.
4. *Ibid.*, p. 72.
5. *Burke's Politics: Selected Writings and Speeches*, Edited by Ross Hoffman and Paul Levack, New York: Alfred A. Knopf, 1949, p. 304.
6. *Utilitarianism, Liberty, and Representative Government*, p. 79.
7. *The Person and the Common Good*, trans. by John J. Fitzgerald. New York: Charles Scribner's Sons, 1942, p. 40.
8. *Burke's Politics*, p. 109.

SELECTED BIBLIOGRAPHY

DOUGLAS, C., *J. S. Mill: A Study of his Philosophy*. Edinburgh.
MacCUNN, J., *Six Radical Thinkers*. London: Longmans.
MURRAY, Robert H., *English Social and Political Thinkers*, Vol. 1. Cambridge: W.
 Heffer & Sons, Ltd.
STEPHEN, FitzJames, *Liberty, Equality, Fraternity*. London.
STEPHEN, Leslie, *The English Utilitarians*. Putnam.
MILL, John Stuart, *Utilitarianism, Liberty, and Representative Government*. Dutton (Everyman's Library).
MILL, John Stuart, *On Liberty*. Regnery.

Thoreau: Civil Disobedience; A Plea for Captain John Brown

It is now a little more than a hundred years since *Civil Disobedience* was written and some ninety years since *A Plea for Captain John Brown* was delivered in Concord Town Hall. A mere decade separates them. Logically they are one. Both are rooted in the same conception of man and hence in the same conception of the origin of political authority, the nature and function of the state. Both develop and apply certain cardinal errors with respect to the social order and its most perfect natural form—the state—that have prevailed under the historic and almost sacrosanct name of Liberalism.

There are those in our time, and they are perhaps much more numerous than their ideological opposites, whose first principles in the social and political order differ not a jot from those of Thoreau. With such it is axiomatic that those states which govern least are the very best; that the state itself is but an expedient, a necessary evil, alien to the nature of man. Even those who accept the "dictatorship of the proletariat" have some vague vision of a stateless society. Obviously Thoreau was not enunciating ideas old and obsolete for modern America.

The point of departure and the basic principles in *Civil Disobedience* constitute the very core of the *Plea* and are today relied upon for truth values and economic values by a large and potent segment of our people. But as so often happens, action and conduct do not entirely conform with basic ideas and first principles. An individualist in the economic order is not an anarchist in the political order. It is no mere coincidence that the intellectual order in America has, in its earnest pursuit of truth, deified chance and contingency, and is confirmed in the belief that such a course has been essential to progress and achievement in the discovery of social patterns and physical laws. Error is thus as much a point of departure as truth. And in the economic order, free enterprise seems to have no effective grammar apart from the optimistic naturalism under the aegis of which Thoreau and his individualistic successors make their analyses of man and society. Out of the wellsprings of Abolition flow also certain of the currents that make for economic servitude.

Thoreau is traditionally regarded as a romantic individualist. He endeavored to reduce life to bare essentials; the production of wealth was to him superfluous; money he could tolerate, but found in no way necessary to man's soul; he followed, for the greater part of his life, no craft or profession; he refused to pay taxes; he neither smoked nor drank; he loved to live the life of a natural recluse in close communion with birds and bees and flowers.

Mysterious and strange are the currents of human thought, and stranger and more mysterious are the winds which blow from so many points to move and trouble the vast waters of man's intellectual existence. The fear of wine and love, the narrow and perverse view of man's social and political nature, the cult of a vague natural mysticism, the almost idolatrous worship of the ego, the denial of man as a discursive social and political creature were not unknown in some proportion to Calvin and Rousseau. The spirit of more than one of their operative ideas hovered over Concord.

Never were occasion and cause more characteristic of the man and the work than in the case of *Civil Disobedience* and its author. When Thoreau refused to pay a tax to his state because it tolerated slavery and when, as a result of such refusal, he was arrested and imprisoned, he proceeded to write an explanation of his action. This explanation, some six years afterward and during the Mexican War, he developed into the discourse now known as *Civil Disobedience*. Payment of the tax would have been on his part a recognition of and allegiance to a government which, he had convinced himself, was promoting and giving legal protection to the institution of slavery. The *Plea* may be more eloquent and moving, but its cardinal ideas are those of *Civil Disobedience*. Both constitute a full and adequate exposition of his social and political theories and the reasoning which supports them.

The main arguments of each are almost identical, are not difficult of digest and summary and are written in a style pointed with obvious paradox—a style in which the art of logic is too often lost in that of rhetoric. A digest and restatement of the principles and the argument on which he proceeds would run as follows:

Government at best is but an expedient. It is rooted in the natural desire of men to be secure from attack and coercion by their fellow men. When it stands aloof from the governed and leaves them alone, it is then most expedient. It is best when it governs not at all.

A government in its endeavor to govern is clearly inexpedient and does not differ from a coercive force such as the standing army which executes its will. Commerce and industry suffer from its attempts at regulation. Social and economic progress it obstructs.

The consent of the governed and mere majority rule do not guarantee political and social justice. Majority rule rests not on justice but on physical strength. Majorities become effective instruments of control and in the process men become mere tools of the state.

The authority of government is of its nature impure. To be strictly just it must have the sanction and consent of the governed. Over the person and property of the individual it can have no pure right unless he actually and formally concedes it.

A democracy such as Americans know is not the last improvement possible in government. It is possible to take a step further toward the recognition and organization of the rights of man. The state must recognize the individual as a higher and independent power from which all power and authority are derived. Refusal of consent on the part of an individual leaves him utterly free and outside the jurisdiction of the state. Disobedience dissolves consent.

Universally men have recognized the right of revolution. American history offers a memorable example of the exercise of this right. Unjust laws, which operate to create injustice of such nature that it requires the individual to be the agent of injustice to another, are invalid and should be violated. Our

American government is at present unjust. It permits slavery and conducts a war of sheer aggression. Therefore, honest citizens should hold aloof from it and pursue a course of disobedience. Our citizens have even a perfect right to interfere by force with the slaveholders in order to rescue the slaves. So far, Thoreau's argument.

The first cardinal error discernible in both *Civil Disobedience* and *A Plea for Captain John Brown* is the conception of the state as an entity external to man's nature, artificial, conventional and merely expedient. Accordingly, it does not develop as an essentially perfect and natural society, which, with numerous smaller communities and, primarily, the family preceding it in a kind of genetic order, has a potential existence in the nature of man. Thoreau obviously omits, because he does not know, any reference to that general mandate of the natural law which obligates man to establish the family and civil society and which furthermore creates the rights and duties that are the essence of the juridical order explicit in such societies.

The juridical origin of society and of the state lies in our human nature. Men are much more dependent than are mere animals. Men need shelter and clothing and food. The physical limitations and needs peculiar to man's bodily existence point to the necessity of society and the state.

Language and laughter and love are essentially human. Each proclaims a nature essentially social. The stateless man is either less or more than a man. But he who is less than a man or more than a man is not a man.

The peace and prosperity of men, the perfection of their human natures, the progress of knowledge and of virtue, cannot be achieved without society and the state. Virtues as well as arts are in many of their operations social. Thus, for Aristotle the state exists for the sake of the good life and not for the sake of life only.

To achieve the good life and perfect their nature, men, actuated by a moral obligation, have established natural societies. Such social forms are so consistent with men's natures and so proportioned thereto and so serve the multifarious desires and demands of that nature that they are essential to its fullness and perfection. But it is demonstrable that men owe their nature and existence to a Creator who is Absolute Act, Absolute

Perfection and whose Reason is the eternal law. It is further demonstrable that there exists in human nature a natural law which participates in this eternal law. The principles of the natural law are self-evident; they order men to the good necessary to the fullness and perfection of their material, moral and intellectual life and the means thereto. Natural societies, such as the family and the state, are among the necessary means. Thus, these social forms are moral necessities reposing on a general mandate of the natural law. Man, created for life in a community, finds in such community the satisfactions and perfections of his nature and is thus acting consistent with that nature and the law which directs that nature to its end.

Thoreau is particularly concerned with the rights of the individual. The state, he points out, must recognize the individual as a higher and independent power from which all power and authority are derived. He is eloquent on the principle that political authority derives its just powers from the sanction and consent of each individual. We must not misconceive the ideas and realities behind his particular use of such memorable terms and phrases. We know that men speak and write and use words and phrases long associated with ideas and principles which they have long since discarded. Witness how the sages of the Enlightenment still used the language of a natural law from which they were utterly separated. The language of Thoreau with respect to individual rights and the origin of political authority is, even in a context which sometimes reads like that of the *Leviathan,* venerable and historic, but the realities which it clothes are not those of the person and his Creator.

The state, to Thoreau and his numerous predecessors, beginning with Hobbes in a limited and qualified way, is the result of contracts between individuals. They not only bring it into existence; they create its obligations and rights. When they obey its mandates, they are merely obeying themselves. They may revoke their consent when they will and thus discard their obligations. This is actually the principle which prevails today with respect to the family and the marriage contract—with most serious peril to our society. Many of our people do not know and certainly do not realize that while the consenting parties as an efficient cause bring into existence the status and the contract, the rights and obligations which are the very essence of marriage flow from a higher order—the natural law.

On the premises under analysis, Thoreau could very readily and logically justify civil disobedience and sedition. Political authority under such premises is envisaged as the utilitarian product of individual self-interest. The common good is then the sum of individual rights and interests. The state has for its proximate end the protection and even the promotion of that liberty which makes for individual self-interest. It is in this light we must consider Thoreau's dictum, there will never be a really free state until the Individual is recognized as a higher and independent power.

There are those who contend that this is the traditional American conception of the state. The Preamble to the Constitution and the principles so memorably set forth in the Declaration do not support the contention. The Preamble is concerned with the promotion of justice and the general welfare as well as with securing the blessings of liberty. It states the common good, which gives form to the United States and its constitution. It is, in brief, an expression of the final cause of the Republic. With respect to the common good and the functions of the state, it does not differ from Suarez's conception of such as the peace and prosperity of the perfect society. Our constitution does not, then, envisage the common good as a service and promotion of the purposes and aims of individuals as such; nor can it be the sum of the individual goods and self-interests of all.

Thus, the United States as a necessary society is under an obligation to promote the welfare of its citizens, as a whole, as members of families and as members of social classes. This is, in brief, the common good; it is not inconsistent with, and it is not actually separated from, the good of individual citizens; but it does not stem from the self-interest of individuals nor is it intended to respond to their desires and demands. It is true that the doctrine of an almost absolute liberty of contract and legislation favorable to special interests has too often repudiated this traditional, necessary and constitutional conception of the common good.

No matter how erroneous the premises and principles on which the political thought of Thoreau leans, we must never forget the dream and vision of the man and the fact that he was one in a long line of native American Liberals, among whom were some of our most effective leaders. That dream and that vision had as its formal principle the truth that not riches but righteousness exalteth a nation.

The second cardinal error in the *Discourse* and the *Plea* springs in the main from the first. Thoreau misconceives an order of law or constitutional government and its operative procedures. He seems to confuse those with mere majority rule. Thus, through a false conception of the origin and nature of political authority; through a confusion of constitutional rule with the tyranny of the majority; through a misconception of liberty, which to him is negative and merely initial, and without any conception of the essential function of authority— which provides for the unity of action of every natural society that cannot, except through common action, attain its common good—he erects the old liberal antinomy absolute and unqualified between liberty and authority. Thus, man is pitted against the state, which in its democratic form becomes majority rule and decision.

The *Discourse* and the *Plea* obviously argue in favor of the necessity of civil disobedience. The argument on which Thoreau proceeds has scant respect, if any at all, for civil authority. He approved the doctrine that the men of his time as individuals had a perfect right to interfere by force with the slaveholders in order to rescue the slaves. This clearly is much more than civil disobedience, much more than passive resistance. It has the element of aggression which we associate with sedition and open revolt. He raised the question as to whether men should endeavor to amend unjust laws and obey them until they had succeeded in amending them, or whether men should at once transgress such laws. His answer was that if such laws so operate that men become agents of injustice to their fellow men, they should not hesitate to violate them. Such doctrines are thoroughly consistent with the premises and principles and the whole background of his political thought.

Now, political authority originates with God. Men freely and instinctively establish the state or body politic. This they do, as we have endeavored to show, under a general mandate of the natural law which, we repeat, is man's participation in the eternal law. Now, political authority is a necessary property of the state or body politic. It rests with the political community and thus, under the natural law, derives from God. Furthermore, it is obvious that since all men are born free and equal, no man or body of men has a right to hold political authority over his equals. Consequently, political authority rests with men as constituents of the state or body politic. But the state or body politic is founded by the consent of its organizing constituents under a general mandate of the natural law. Therefore, political authority, though rooted in the people and the body politic, has its source in nature and consequently in God, the author of nature. Thus in the main runs the historic but cogent and logical argument of Suarez's in *De Legibus III*.

Now, since political authority emanates from God, the most august and holy of all sources; since it is rooted in the people, and since they through their consent bring into existence a political community to which they give form and authority, they must, in the words of the Encyclical *Diuturnum Illud,*

". . . shun sedition and rebellion, for the conviction must possess them that whoever resists the authority of the state resists an authority that is Divine; that whoever refuses honor to rulers, refuses to honor God Himself."

An essentially bad rule operated by a tyrant or usurper does not command the obedience and honor so nobly enunciated in the Encyclical. It is obvious that when a law or an order or a command openly conflicts with the natural law or the law of God, a refusal to obey is absolutely just. This principle applies not only to the citizen in relation to his government but to the child in relation to its parents. On this principle, the early Christians refused to worship Caesar and bore witness to this refusal and to the Faith by their blood and thus were numbered among the Martyrs.

Through the Middle Ages and all through true Christian thought there is an all-but-unanimous recognition of the right of disobedience and the right of resistance to—and open revolt in particular circumstances against—tyrants and usurpers and forms of government which in their operations have become essentially bad. Charter after charter in the Middle Ages—principal among them the Great Charter—recognized in the people the right to revolt when kings and princes do not fulfill the obligations which they had sworn to observe. However, it must not escape us that St. Thomas *(De Regimine Principum)* and Suarez *(Defensio Fidei)* insist that the initiation and execution of action against an essentially bad rule, against the cruelties and terror of a tyrant, rest with the public or their representatives, such as the nobles and the cities during the Middle Ages, and not with individuals.

Now, Thoreau was not confronted with a usurper or a tyrant or an essentially bad government. It is true that a particular form of injustice permeated a large segment of the society in which he lived, and the evil was increasing. The condition was serious, but not general as it was in the Roman Empire at the advent of the Faith, and it certainly was not beyond amelioration and ultimate eradication by other means than a resort to arms. But the passionately righteous Thoreau in his campaign against the evil did not stop at civil disobedience or passive resistance; he agreed with and sanctioned in the *Plea* the aggressive course of action followed by Captain John Brown.

The vice of the principles which actuated Thoreau's campaign was sheer individualism. Anarchy rather than reform would have been the probable result of his passionate appeals had they been translated into action. The right of the people to their own common good would not have been promoted. It is essential that whenever the issue of disobedience or passive resistance or open revolt against even an essentially bad rule arises, the primary and decisive consideration should be the common good. The moral criteria which in theory justify open revolt and recourse to arms against a tyrant support this. They revolve around the common good. One essential condition is necessity. The rule against which resistance and revolt are directed must be substantially and habitually tyrannical, defeating the right of the people to their own common good. Another essential condition, the chance of success, is clearly related to the common good. Prudence dictates that unsuccessful revolt and resistance would leave the people with respect to peace and prosperity and general justice in a much worse condition than they were under the tyrant before the inception of the revolt. It is also obvious that injustices of a particular rather than a general nature cannot justify recourse to violent means, since one cannot disturb public order and endanger peace and prosperity unless the common good is in grave and imminent peril.

One may add that—under a constitutional rule whose cornerstone is the doctrine of natural rights, due process of law and the procedures incident thereto—reform of economic and political conditions, the operation of social justice and the elimination of injustices attain a comparative success. Thus the necessity not only for revolution but for civil disobedience and passive resistance disappears. It is one of the ironies of history that when sedition and revolt came, they did not come because of the dream and vision for which Thoreau pleaded, and that the constitutional rule, Federal and state, which he so passionately denounced, championed his cause and achieved certain of his aims against sedition and revolt. One cannot fail to read, in the historic events surrounding Abolition and the Civil War, the tragic frailty which blinded Thoreau at the crossroads of decision.

THOMAS P. WHELAN

SELECTED BIBLIOGRAPHY

HUGHES, Philip, *The Pope's New Order*. Macmillan.
LECLERCQ, Jacques, *Leçons De Droit Naturel*, Second Edition, Revised, Volume 2. Paris: Société d'Études Morales.
MASON, Alpheus Thomas, *Free Government in the Making*. Oxford.
ROMMEN, Heinrich A., *The State in Catholic Thought*. Herder.
SIMON, Yves R., *Nature and Functions of Authority*. Marquette University Press.
THOREAU, Henry David, *Works*, Selected and edited by H. S. Canby. Houghton, Mifflin.
THOREAU, Henry David, *Walden and Other Writings*. Random House (Modern Library).
THOREAU, Henry David, *Civil Disobedience; A Plea for Captain John Brown.* Regnery.

Freud: The Origin and Development
of Psychoanalysis

THESE ARE FIVE lectures which Freud gave before the Department of Psychology of Clark University in 1909 on the occasion of the University's twentieth anniversary. How startled the audience must have been to hear observations and conclusions so novel and revolutionary!

I wonder if there is any other field that is so uniquely the product of one man's genius. Freud himself generously gives credit for the origin of psychoanalysis to Breuer, an internist, who was working out in a remarkable way the dynamics of the symptomatology of a young woman hysteric at a time when Freud was just a medical student. Not long afterward Freud and Breuer associated for a while and collaborated in the first and epochal paper in the field, *Studien über Hysterie.* Why Breuer, who must have been blessed with the specific genius to unravel the particular mysteries of the field of neuroses, discontinued his investigations is cause for speculation. Freud himself ascribed this to a resistance occasioned by the bringing to light of hidden sexual material. At any rate, Freud continued on his own to pursue the new science of psychoanalysis, to make many profound and penetrating clinical observations, to develop a masterly technical procedure, to build hypotheses and theories and to apply his new science to other fields such as art, literature, anthropology and religion.

Breuer's patient, a young woman, suffered from hysteria, a disorder having no organic foundation, which manifested itself in her case in a multiplicity of bizarre symptoms, such as paralyses, anesthesias, inability to drink water, nausea and confused states. In her conscious state she was unable to afford any explanation of her difficulties or to throw any light on them.

The great discovery Breuer made was that under hypnosis she could be made to recall certain traumatic incidents whose relationship to the symptoms in question had been forgotten, "repressed." Only with the bringing to light of this connection did the symptom become meaningful as a symbol, a precipitate, a "monument" of the original disturbing episode. In this process there was released a strong emotion which had been evoked by the original situation and had also been subject to repression. With the meaning of the symptom now known to the patient, and with the appropriate emotion that had been originally aroused now released, the symptom disappeared. The patient, through the new technic, had been able to complete a psychological task that had hitherto remained unfinished and unavailable.

Freud quickly became dissatisfied with the hypnotic method and developed as his own unique contribution the psychoanalytic technic. He found he could obtain the repressed material more effectively through observation and analysis of slips, symptomatic acts and errors of everyday life and (much more important) through analysis of dreams (the royal road to the unconscious), free association and the elucidation of the phenomenon of transference.

The thoughts that came to the patient in his free associations were surrogates, allusions, indirect expressions of the sought-for repressed ideas. The continuation of the process eventually made it possible to understand what had hitherto been hidden.

During the treatment the patient expressed intense emotional attitudes toward the analyst that in no way were explainable on the basis of the analyst's attitudes or behavior. Freud discovered that these emotional responses were repetitions of attitudes that had formerly been expressed to persons (such as parents) of key significance in the patient's life. The elucidation of the patient's "transferred" attitudes to the analyst helped recall the original, past, repressed attitudes that had been so significant in molding the patient's character and forming his symptoms. To this process Freud gave the name "transference."

Freud discovered that the repressed material of basic importance in the creation of symptoms was not only of a sexual nature but of an "infantilely" sexual nature. Sex was used by Freud not in its ordinary meaning but for all the libidinal pleasure strivings which had their inception in earliest infantile life. The organization of libido went through successive transformations to an eventual mature organization. Disturbances in this developmental process, with fixations at some immature stage, were considered basic in the creation of neuroses. Furthermore, relationships were discovered between the various neuroses and fixations at specific levels of libidinal development.

Before proceeding to comments about Freud's findings, it must be emphasized that what has been so far said is hardly more than a mere glimpse at the structure Freud created. Without a fairly comprehensive knowledge of psychoanalysis—and particularly without clinical experience—it is hardly possible to pass judgment.

The underlying basic concept clearly expressed even in Freud's earliest work is that of psychic determinism, the concept that any phenomenon of mental life, whether it be a delusion, an hysterical paralysis, a dream, a slip of the tongue, or free association, is not a chance occurrence but the result of interacting forces and consequently capable of being analyzed. It is only because of this primary attitude that analysis has developed and can exist as a fruitful investigative and curative process.

The technic of psychoanalysis which Freud originated as involving both investigation and therapy (elements which can never be separated) has remained a more and more validly established process. Those who have used it have amply confirmed Freud's findings of an unconscious mental life, of hidden conflicting trends within the personality existing in a kind of independent life, not subject to control or modification, surcharged with strong feelings, motivating the patient's behavior and determining character structure and symptom formation. There has been the most ample confirmation that the therapeutic process struggles against the resistance of the patient to undo what has been accomplished by repression. It is due to the genius of Freud that a present-day analyst can succeed in understanding and coping with the defensive systems of the patient and in bringing to light the hidden forces and conflicts motivating the patient. There has been the most ample confirmation that even more important in the therapeutic process than this uncovering, this bringing of the hidden into light, more important than the patient's gaining of insight, is the analysis and working through of the transference, the emotional attitudes established by the patient toward his analyst.

It is most important to bear in mind that psychoanalysis did not originate as a speculation or philosophical inquiry. It began with clinical investigation and therapeutic effort. It did not spring into existence in Freud's mind as a finished vision complete in every detail. With further investigation new observations were made, new questions came to light and modifications were made in the theories constructed to explain the accumulated data. Freud himself on several occasions changed his concepts. For example, he discovered that what he had thought to be real incidents uncovered from the patient's early past were sometimes only phantasies. He first thought that only repressed sexual strivings were the cause of anxiety, but he later realized his error in not having seen the importance of repressed hostile drives.

Theories are useful insofar as they effectively lead us into new investigations and findings. They are hindrances when they become so rigid and fixed as to stultify new approaches and new investigations. Though there is not now universal acceptance by analysts of all of Freud's postulates, there has been the most convincing confirmation of the castration complex, the Oedipus complex and other manifestations of disturbed sexual development that Freud had first observed. However, many analysts do not ascribe to sexuality the preeminent role in the etiology of neuroses that Freud did. They do not hold with his libido theory, nor with his concepts of anxiety and personality structure. An example of detailed, far-reaching and yet constructive criticism of Freud can be found in the writings of Karen Horney. She looks upon a neurosis as the culmination of a neurotic character structure set up in childhood as the result of inimical circumstances, especially nonloving and neurotic attitudes in the parents. These cause the child to feel helpless in a hostile world, a world that is unloving, rejecting, thwarting, squelching, etc. It is from this background that (basic) anxiety originates and rigid defensive maneuvers (isolation, compulsive compliance, etc.) are established in the search for security. These maneuvers, rigid and unwholesome, in turn may arouse resentment, hostility, envy, etc. and increase basic anxiety and aggravate the need to seek safety neurotically. The neurotic patterns set up in childhood are not perceived as such by the patient. In the transfer-

FREUD: PSYCHOANALYSIS 151

ence, the analyst is not assigned the role of mother or father but rather is the recipient of the patient's attitudes springing from the neurotic life-pattern he has established, as for example, trends toward being subservient to the analyst, belittling him, being hostile to him, etc.

There are several highly controversial issues in psychoanalysis, with different groups favoring special formulations. The existence of controversy is not cause for alarm. It can be beneficial in creating a pressure for an ever more precise, correct and fruitful formulation. Quite likely, though, a certain amount of overemphasis and overexaggeration of special formulations has occurred.

At any rate, as a medical discipline (and similar to all the other medical disciplines) psychoanalysis is not a closed and finished product, nor was it ever so presented by Freud, but a changing, growing body of knowledge and technics. One of the most significant of recent contributions is in the field of psychosomatic medicine.

As the essential originator, creator and developer of a new investigative and curative medical procedure, psychoanalysis, Freud has made a monumental contribution. There is hardly any type of functional emotional disorder or aspect of mental life that has not been powerfully illuminated by his genius.

Even greater is the sum-total of his contribution when account is taken of the various nonmedical applications of psychoanalysis which Freud also initiated. Pedagogy, artistic and literary criticism, anthropology, criminology, sociology, all have been influenced by Freud's work. However, as is often the case with a man entering fields other than his own with insufficient humility, Freud's applications of his method and results, particularly in anthropology and religion, have been seriously erroneous and much critized by experts in those fields.

It seems so strange that Freud, with his great genius for seeing what others before him had never seen, was himself incapable of seeing what so many people even without any genius had seen before him. He denied God. Lacking faith, he had no way of fitting his findings into the vast framework of God's design for man. Not accepting God's plan for us, he had no plan to put in its place. His insistence on the neutral attitude of the analyst toward the patient's problems; the necessity of the analyst for refraining from interjecting his own standards and philosophy and for helping the patient attain the most advantageous position from which to struggle with the problems of life, but without holding out specific goals and ideals to him, without influencing him in any direction—all this was a logical outcome of Freud's own ignorance of what the goal of life was. Some analysts, like Horney and Zilboorg, while accepting in varying degrees Freud's scientific findings, reject his false philosophy, while other analysts share with Freud his antireligious bias.

The antireligious bias that has contaminated psychoanalysis has done great harm. Freud postulated as an aim of psychoanalysis not the "release" (meaning unconditional gratification) of repressed drives but their control. But control is not so effective when no specific criteria of behavior are acknowledged in terms of God's laws for us. Just what "gratifications" are permissible? Just what kind of controls should be aimed for? It is obvious that faith, a belief in Divine Law and in the controls God wishes us to establish, will make easier the task of bringing inner impulses under control.

Further, what does a psychoanalysis without faith have for alleviating the suffering of humanity that is not neurotically determined? Without faith, psychoanalysis can answer none of the basic problems of life. For one who has lost a loved one or is himself about to die, there is not a crumb of consolation in the writings of Freud. Lacking faith, Freud would have robbed the world of the correct and wonderful answers it already possessed.

Analysis can help to remove neurotic elements in suffering. It can stop a patient from unconsciously imposing suffering upon himself or bringing it upon himself through his neurotic mechanisms, and it can remove neurotic guilt, but there still remains the real suffering, which is not a neurotic by-product and which no one can escape. How curious it is that the psychoanalysis which can help the neurotic extricate himself from his unhappy, neurotic state would rob him, when it lacks faith, of the means of effectively dealing with the unhappy difficulties that come to his adjusted, nonneurotic personality.

Again, where in our quest for adjustment and security shall psychoanalysis have us stop? Psychoanalysis helps us attain better adjustment and greater security, but it is only faith that enables us to find the ultimate in both.

Psychoanalysis is curative, because whatever hurts the patient has received in life can be undone in the healthier, more satisfying relationship held out to him by the analyst. An individual who was unloved and consequently hates and so inspires reciprocal hatred in others will, in the transference, hate his analyst, but the analyst will respond not with reciprocal hatred but with a persistent understanding and love which will eventually teach the patient he can be loved and which will inspire him to show love himself. Yes, analysis can do this, but how much more is done when an individual will enter into the relationship God holds out to him! How sad is the spectacle of a psychoanalysis without faith, offering humanity a little bit in one hand and with the other taking away everything. There is nothing wrong morally with psychoanalysis as such. All that is wrong is the anti-religious bias that has contaminated it, a contamination that resulted not from any clinical observations but from the false philosophy that was Freud's as he began and pursued his work.

FREDERICK ROSENHEIM

SELECTED BIBLIOGRAPHY

FREUD, Sigmund, *A General Introduction to Psychoanalysis*. Garden City.
HORNEY, Karen, *New Ways in Psychoanalysis*. Norton.
ST. JOHN OF THE CROSS, *The Ascent of Mt. Carmel*. Newman.
ZILBOORG, "Psychoanalysis and Religion," *Atlantic Monthly*, Jan., 1949.
FREUD, Sigmund, *The Origin and Development of Psychoanalysis*. Regnery.

Notes on the Contributors

Rev. Rudolph Arbesmann, O.S.A. [1895-   ]

After early education in his natal Fürth, Germany, Father Arbesmann attended the Universities of Würzburg, Munich and Rome. He was ordained in Rome in 1923 and received his doctorate at the University of Würzburg in 1929. That same year he sat for the state examination in classics, history and Germanic languages at the same university. He was assistant professor of classics at the Humanistisches Gymnasium at Münnerstadt, Bavaria (1930-1931), and at the International College St. Monica, Rome (1931-1934), and professor of ancient history and archeology at the Universitad Católica, Santiago, Chile (1934-1937). Coming to the United States, he was appointed assistant professor of classics at Fordham in 1937 and has been associate professor since 1944. He is the author of three volumes in German on classical subjects, and in addition to contributing to German encyclopedias, he also writes frequently for such journals as the *Classical Weekly, Classical Bulletin, Traditio, Thought, The Americas.* He is coeditor of the series entitled Fathers of the Church, published by Fathers of the Church, Inc., New York.

André J. de Béthune [1919-   ]

Dr. de Béthune, born in Brussels of an eminent political, scholarly and military family, came to the United States in 1928. He received his B.S. degree from St. Peter's College and his Ph.D. in Physical Chemistry from Columbia University. For several years he was associated with the Manhattan Atomic Bomb Project and later was National Research Fellow at the Massachusetts Institute of Technology. At present he is Associate Professor of Chemistry at Boston College. Dr. de Béthune has done extensive research in electrochemistry, the kinetic theory of gases and catalysis, and is the author of several papers in scientific literature.

Charles A. Brady [1912-   ]

Mr. Brady, winner of the Archbishop Cushing Award for Poetry, 1949, is Chairman of the English Department at Canisius College, Buffalo, and weekly book columnist for the Buffalo *Evening News.* He is the author of *Cat Royal* (Sheed & Ward) and was the editor of *A Catholic Reader* (Desmond & Stapleton). During the winter of 1950-1951, Mr. Brady will have two volumes published: *Valentine for Toby: Poems,* and *Reclaim Imagination: A Critique on C. S. Lewis and Charles Williams.* Besides writing reviews for various magazines, he is a frequent contributor of articles and poems to *America, Thought, Renascence, Catholic World, Saturday Review of Literature, Best Sellers* and *Harvard Advocate.*

REV. WILLIAM ALOYSIUS DOWD, S.J. [1884-   ]

Father Dowd, born in Cincinnati, received his primary education from the Sisters of Charity in Springer Institute and his higher training in Xavier University, with the degree of A.B. in 1905. Joining the Jesuits the same year, he followed their regular course at Florissant, Missouri, and at St. Louis University, receiving his A.M. in 1912. After a year of special study and teaching at Florissant, he taught the classics for four years at St. Mary's College, Kansas. He studied theology for four years at St. Louis University, being ordained there in 1920. Three years at the Biblical Institute, Rome, were succeeded by tertianship at Tullamore, Ireland. From 1925 to the present he has been professor of Sacred Scripture at St. Mary of the Lake Seminary, Mundelein, Illinois. He has published *Memory Gems* (1918), *Loyola Latin Elements* (1920), and *The Gospel Guide* (1932) and has contributed book reviews to various Catholic publications, especially to *America*.

REV. HAROLD C. GARDINER, S.J. [1902-   ]

A native of Washington, D. C., Father Gardiner entered the Society of Jesus in 1922. After classical studies at St. Andrew-on-Hudson, Poughkeepsie, N. Y., philosophical studies at Woodstock College, Woodstock, Md., a period of teaching the classics and English at Canisius College, Buffalo, N. Y., he returned to Woodstock for theological studies and ordination. A year of ascetical theology in Belgium was succeeded by his entering Downing College, Cambridge University, for postgraduate work in English. The outbreak of the war forced his return to the United States in 1940, but he was able to receive his Ph.D. from Cambridge *in absentia* in 1941. Since 1940 he has been Literary Editor of *America*. He is also Editorial Chairman of the Catholic Book Club and of the Catholic Children's Book Club. His published work, in addition to articles and reviews in *America* and other periodicals, includes *Mysteries End*, a study of the cessation of the medieval religious stage (Yale University Press, 1945), *Tenets for Readers and Reviewers* (America Press, 1942, 1947). The series of articles on the Great Books comprising this volume are a continuation of a series which appeared originally under his editorship in *America*.

WILLIAM JOSEPH GRACE [1910-   ]

Mr. Grace received his Bachelor's degree from Balliol College, Oxford, in 1933, and his Master's degree in 1937. He has taught and lectured at St. Bonaventure's College, Olean, New York; Fordham University; the Seminary of the Immaculate Conception, Huntington, Long Island, and the College of Notre Dame, Staten Island. He is a contributor to reviews and quarterlies, among them *America, Commonweal, Thought, Sewanee Review,* the *Journal of the History of Ideas.* He at present teaches English at Fordham University's School of Education. Mr. Grace is also a contributor to Volume I in this series on the Great Books.

REV. BERNARD A. HAUSMANN [1899-   ]

A native of Cleveland, Ohio, Father Hausmann entered the Society of Jesus at Florissant, Mo., in 1918. He received an M.A. degree from Gonzaga University in 1925 and his doctorate in mathematics from Yale University in 1937. He was chairman of the department of mathematics at the University of Detroit from 1937 to 1944. He is professor of mathematics and the philosophy of mathematics at West Baden College, West Baden Springs, Indiana.

DIETRICH VON HILDEBRAND [1889-   ]

Born in Florence October 12, 1889, Dr. von Hildebrand crowned his early studies with a doctorate degree at Goettingen in 1912. He taught at the University of Munich from 1919 to 1933. Hitler's rise to power forced him to Vienna, where he was a professor at the university until 1938. He was founder and editor of the Catholic anti-Nazi magazine *Der Christliche Standestaat*. Repudiating Nazism once again, he went to Toulouse as professor at the Catholic University, 1939-1940, and finally came to the United States. He has been Professor of Philosophy at Fordham University since 1941 and has become an American citizen. In addition to many works in German, he is author of *In Defense of Purity, Liturgy and Personality, Transformation in Christ, Marriage* and *Fundamental Moral Attitudes*. Dr. von Hildebrand has contributed to the first two volumes of the Great Books series.

REV. DOMINIC HUGHES, O.P. [1918-   ]

Father Hughes, besides his Bachelor of Arts degree from Providence College, has a Lectorate in Sacred Theology from the Dominican Order. He obtained his Doctorate in Sacred Theology in Rome at the Pontifical Faculty, the Angelicum, in 1947. A former editor of *The Thomist*, he contributes to other Catholic periodicals. He is Professor of Moral and Mystical Theology at the Dominican Pontifical Faculty of Theology in Washington, D. C. His lecturing, especially his series in Theology for the Laity, has been heard principally in eastern cities.

SISTER MARY IRMA, B.V.M.

Professor of English and moderator of literary publications at Mundelein College, Sister Mary Irma entered the Congregation of the Sisters of Charity of the Blessed Virgin Mary after her graduation from Clarke College. She became interested in Milton while attending the lectures of Frank Allen Patterson at Columbia University, where she received her M.A., and later resumed her Renaissance studies at the Catholic University of America, writing her doctoral dissertation, *Milton's Paradise with Reference to the Hexameral Background,* under the direction of Dr. Kerby Neill. In 1948 she was co-recipient of the *Atlantic Monthly* scholarships to the Bread Loaf School of English awarded to Patricia Kiely for her prize-winning short story. Her avocation is the writing of verse, which has appeared in various periodicals.

REV. WILLIAM F. LYNCH, S.J. [1908-   ]

Father Lynch is the present editor of *Thought,* the Fordham University Quarterly, and member of the Philosophy Department of the Graduate School.

A graduate of Fordham College, he served a year as a reporter on the editorial staff of The New York *Herald Tribune.* In 1931 he returned to Fordham as an instructor in Greek and philosophy, and three years later entered the Society of Jesus. During the traditional teaching period of the Jesuit scholastic he became absorbed in the study of theatrical production and was the director responsible for the series of classical plays done at Fordham from 1940-1942: including streamlined versions of the *Aulularia* of Plautus, the *Clouds* of Aristophanes, the *Bourgeois Gentilhomme* of Molière, and full-length productions of the *Oedipus Rex* and the *Eumenides*. During his theological studies at Weston College, Weston, Mass., he dramatized parts of the *Canterbury Tales* and did a modernized version of *Everyman*. His primary interest has always been Platonism. He has just completed the manuscript of a book called *The Metaphysics of Plato*: a summary in the form of a commentary on the *Parmenides*. He has published articles in *America, Spirit, The Modern Schoolman, The Jesuit Educational Quarterly* and *Liturgical Arts*.

JEAN PAUL MISRAHI [1910-   ]

Columbia University granted Dr. Misrahi his A.B. in 1929 and his doctorate in 1933. He has studied at the Universities of Paris and Nancy. He was an instructor in Romance languages at Brooklyn College from 1933 to 1938. Since 1938 he has been Assistant Professor and then Associate Professor, and was Head of the Department of Romance Languages at Fordham University Graduate School from 1938 to 1948. He is a contributor to *Liturgical Arts, Speculum, The French Review* and other magazines. He is a member of the editorial board of *Thought* and the author of *Le Roman des Sept Sages*. Dr. Misrahi is among the contributors to Volumes I and II of this series on the Great Books.

DR. CHARLES J. O'NEIL [1908-   ]

Dr. O'Neil received his B.A. from St. Louis University in 1932 and his M.A. from the same University the following year. He prepared his doctorate at Toronto's Institute of Medieval Studies, and was awarded the degree of Ph.D. in 1939. During this period he also held the Rev. W. L. Murray Memorial Fellowship in Medieval Philosophy. He was an instructor in philosophy at Loyola University in Chicago for the periods 1934-1936 and 1939-1941, when he was awarded an assistant-professorship in the same department. In 1942 he was commissioned as instructor of ground cadets in the A.A.F. and later, 1945-1946, was an education officer in the India-Burma theater. He was discharged from the Army in January 1946 and joined the Faculty of the Graduate School, Marquette University, in 1947. He has contributed articles and reviews to *New Scholasticism* and *The Modern Schoolman*. His best known work is *Essays in Thomism*.

REV. PACIFICO A. ORTIZ, S.J. [1913-   ]

Father Ortiz made his classical, philosophical and theological studies at the Jesuit Seminary in Manila, Philippines, and received his S.T.L. from Woodstock College, Maryland. Before the war he taught philosophy at the Ateneo de Manila, Philippines. During the war he served as chaplain on Corregidor and later as personal chaplain to the late President Quezon of the Philippines. He is at present working for his Ph.D. degree in political philosophy at Fordham University. Father Ortiz was a contributor to Volume II of the present series.

REV. EDWIN A. QUAIN, S.J. [1906-   ]

Father Quain's college degrees of A.B. and M.A. were obtained at Woodstock College, Maryland. His S.T.L. is from the same institution, in 1937. His doctorate in the classics was granted by Harvard University in 1941. From 1941 to 1945 he was an instructor in the classics in the Fordham University Graduate School; since 1945 he has been an assistant professor in the same subject. He is Editor of the Fordham University Studies and of *Traditio* (Studies in Ancient and Medieval History, Thought and Religion). He is a contributor to *America, Traditio,* the *Classical Bulletin, Thought* and *Speculum*. He is author of the translation of Tertullian *On The Soul* in *The Fathers of the Church in Translation* and of "The Medieval Accessus ad Auctores," *Traditio* III, 215-264. Father Quain contributed to Volumes I and II of this series on the Great Books.

HEINRICH ROMMEN [1897-   ]

Dr. Rommen studied at the Universities of Muenster, Munich and Bonn, receiving from the last the degree of J.U.D. He was Director of the Social Action Department of Volks-Verein at Gladbach, and of Brandts-Hilze House School for Politics and Economics. After being Chairman of the National Catholic Committee for Civic Education, Dr. Rommen was imprisoned by the Nazis. He came to America following his release and now teaches at the College of St. Thomas, St. Paul, Minnesota. He is the author of *Political Theory of Fr. Suarez, S.J.* (Gladbach), *The Bills of Rights and the Supremacy of the Judiciary* (Muenster), *In Defense of Canon Law* (Gladbach), *The State* (Paderborn), *On Natural Law* (Leipzig), *The State in Catholic Thought* (Herder) and *The Natural Law* (translated by Fr. Thomas Hanley, O.S.B., Herder) and has contributed articles to *Nova et Vetera* (Fribourg) and *Review of Politics* (Notre Dame).

FREDERICK J. P. ROSENHEIM, M.D. [1907-   ]

Dr. Rosenheim received his B.A. and M.D. degrees at Columbia College, New York, and took his psychiatric training at Kings Park State Hospital, Central Islip State Hospital, and New York Psychoanalytic Institute. Until 1949 he was co-director of the Judge Baker Guidance Center in Boston. At present he is professor of Psychiatry at the Boston College School of Social Work, and engages in private practice of psychiatry and psychoanalysis. Dr. Rosenheim is a member of the Massachusetts Medical Society, the American Orthopsychiatric Association, the Boston Psychoanalytic Society, and the American Psychoanalytic Association.

REV. EDWARD A. RYAN, S.J. [1900-   ]

Father Ryan received his education at Canisius College, Boston College, Gonzaga University and the University of Louvain, and was ordained at Dublin in 1931. He was Instructor in history at Loyola College, Baltimore, and at present is Professor of Church History at Woodstock College. Father Ryan is the author of *The Historical Scholarship of St. Bellarmine* (Louvain).

REV. GUSTAVE WEIGEL, S.J. [1906-   ]

Father Weigel's A.B. and M.A. are from Woodstock College, Woodstock, Md. Following his ordination in 1934, he went to Rome for graduate ecclesiastical studies. He received the degree of S.T.D. from the Gregorian University in 1938. For eleven years following he was prominent in the academic life of Chile, where he was professor of philosophy and theology and Dean of the School of Divinity of the Catholic University of Chile. Since 1948 he has been professor of Ecclesiology at Woodstock College. He has written several works in Spanish and was the founder of the *Anales de la Facultad de Teología,* an annual review of theology. Father Weigel was a contributor to Volume II of this series.

THOMAS P. WHELAN [1897-   ]

Dr. Whelan received his college education in Ireland and Scotland. He is a graduate of the Gregorian University, Rome. He did graduate work at the University of Pittsburgh and from that institution received his Master's degree in 1923. From Marquette University Law School, he received his J.D. in 1927. He has studied at the Gaelic colleges in the west of Ireland and is deeply interested in the Irish language and in Irish literature. He is a member of the Milwaukee and Wisconsin Bar Associations and of the National Academy of Arbitrators. During World War II he served for some three years as a public panel member of the War Labor Board. He is a member of the Conciliation and Arbitration Panel established by the Wisconsin Employment Relations Board. Among the reviews and periodicals to which he has contributed are: the *Wisconsin Law Review,* the *Marquette Law Review,* the *Irish Monthly,* and the *Irish Ecclesiastical Record.* He is, at present, a Professor on the faculty of Marquette University.